Writing History

THIRD EDITION

A GUIDE FOR CANADIAN STUDENTS

WILLIAM KELLEHER STOREY
TOWSER JONES

P9-CPY-644

OXFORD

UNIVERSITY PRESS

OXFORD
UNIVERSITY PRESS

8 Sampson Mews, Suite 204, Don Mills, Ontario M3C 0H5
www.oupcanada.com

Oxford University Press is a department of the University of Oxford. It furthers the University's
objective of excellence in research, scholarship, and education by publishing worldwide in

Oxford   New York
Auckland   Cape Town   Dar es Salaam   Hong Kong   Karachi   Kuala Lumpur   Madrid
Melbourne   Mexico City   Nairobi   New Delhi   Shanghai   Taipei   Toronto

With offices in
Argentina   Austria   Brazil   Chile   Czech Republic   France   Greece
Guatemala   Hungary   Italy   Japan   Poland   Portugal   Singapore
South Korea   Switzerland   Thailand   Turkey   Ukraine   Vietnam

Oxford is a trade mark of Oxford University Press in the UK and in certain other countries

Published in Canada by Oxford University Press

Library and Archives Canada Cataloguing in Publication

Storey, William Kelleher
Writing history : a guide for Canadian students / William Kelleher Storey,
Towser Jones. — 3rd ed.

Includes bibliographical references and index.
ISBN 978-0-19-544012-6

1. History—Research. 2. History—Research—Canada.
3. Academic writing. 4. Historiography.
5. Historiography—Canada. I. Jones, Towser II. Title.

D16.S76 2011   907.2   C2011-901526-9

Cover image: Joel Addams/Aurora Collection, Getty Images

MIX
Paper from
responsible sources
FSC® C004071

Oxford University Press is committed to our environment. The pages of this book have been
printed on paper which has been certified by the Forest Stewardship Council®.

2   3   4   –   14   13   12   11

৩ CONTENTS ৩

✍ Preface to the Third ✍ Canadian Edition

William Kelleher Storey's book *Writing History* had its origins in the Harvard Writing Project and was first published by Oxford University Press in 1999. Following the success of his second edition, Oxford asked me to write a Canadian adaptation (2003; revised 2008).

Why would we need yet another Canadian edition of this text? It's true that Canadians are accustomed to reading books from elsewhere; in fact, we are increasingly exhorted to see Canada as part of a global culture. On the other hand, it is still important to recognize the Canadian context and the unique aspects of the Canadian experience, including Canadian history. It is also important to recognize how the needs of students continue to change.

Preparing this third edition has been both a pleasure and a challenge. Though I've tried to preserve Storey's informal tone and practical approach, the text has been extensively reorganized and updated, with expanded coverage of electronic resources and Canadian research materials, as well as additional examples that should have particular meaning to Canadian students. There are many excellent Canadian historians, and I hope this edition will serve as an introduction to at least a few of them.

As always, I am delighted to honour my debts. Mary Wat at Oxford was a pleasure to work with, supportive and enormously helpful. Sally Livingston, my resourceful editor, saved me from a variety of errors and problems. Six anonymous reviewers offered useful advice, much of which I followed. Any errors that remain, of course, are not their fault. Friends and colleagues at Capilano University, particularly Dean Robert Campbell and Nanci Lucas and Denis Dubord of the history department, offered encouragement and ideas. I am also very grateful to my former student Justin Elsworth, who generously allowed me to use extracts from some of his papers as examples. Finally, and as always, my most profound thanks go to my family, Don, Katriona, Rob, Max, and Jake—"the wind beneath my wings" doesn't even begin to cover it.

⁓ INTRODUCTION ⁓

What is history? No single definition is universally accepted, but historians do generally agree on several points. History is not a compilation of names and dates to be memorized and regurgitated. Nor is it the simple description of "what happened" in the past. History is not a matter of right and wrong answers. It reflects the time in which it is written. It demands critical analysis, questioning and exploration, selection, debate, and interpretation.

Historians study the human past, ancient and recent, to understand not only what happened, but how and why, what it means and why it matters. And it does matter. Understanding the past gives us a basis for understanding the present. In the words of the Canadian historian Margaret MacMillan, "history is not a dead subject. . . . [It] lies under the present, silently shaping our institutions, our ways of thought, our likes and dislikes."[1] Historians seek to understand the significance of past events and people not only in their own times, but also in the present. Not surprisingly, historians frequently disagree with one another. Thus Louis Riel has been seen as a villain and a hero, a champion of Aboriginal and of Francophone rights, a misunderstood genius and a lunatic. Such debates are so common that there is a whole subfield of the discipline called **historiography**, the study of writing history—in a sense, the history of history.

Writing history is about making decisions. First, historians choose the subjects they think are most important. Then they choose the source materials they judge most likely to shed useful light on those subjects. After carefully analyzing all the evidence they can find, they develop arguments and draw conclusions in the light of that evidence. Finally, they choose how they will present their arguments in writing so as to balance respect for their subjects with the needs of their readers.

The best historians are so skilled at making choices that they can transform painstaking research into seamless arguments and narratives. But don't be fooled. The process of writing is filled with difficult decisions. Even with the best sources and methods, writing history can be like trying to "nail jelly to a wall".[2] For this reason, historians experiment with many approaches to the past, although in the end they must choose an approach that suits their subject.

Selection has been central to Western historical writing ever since the time of the ancient Greeks. When the Athenian general Thucydides composed his history of the Peloponnesian Wars, around 400 BCE, he could hardly report everything that had taken place over thirty years of battles and defeats. Instead, he chose to focus on decisive moments. Among the latter was the famous eulogy for the Athenian dead delivered by the statesman and general Pericles:

> I have no wish to make a long speech on subjects familiar to you all: so I shall say nothing about the warlike deeds by which we acquired our power or the battles in which we or our fathers gallantly resisted our enemies, Greek or foreign. What I want to do is, in the first place, to discuss the spirit in which we faced our trials and also our constitution and the way of life which has made us great. After that I shall speak in praise of the dead. . . .[3]

Thucydides chose to make Pericles' speech a part of his history not just because he found it moving, but because he believed it to be instructive on the nature of Athenian democracy.

Like Thucydides, modern-day historians also tend to choose subjects that they believe to be relevant to contemporary circumstances. In response to a recent debate on the value of teaching Canadian history, for instance, Ruth Sandwell, a specialist in the history of education, edited a collection of essays exploring "history education, public memory, and citizenship in Canada." Sandwell and her contributors linked their concerns about the current teaching of history in Canadian schools to "some of the deeper problems that we, as a society, have about how knowledge, identity and power are created and sustained within our social system."[4]

Like Thucydides, historians also choose subjects that they believe can shed light on the causes of change over time. To that end, they must learn how to find sources, how to report on them faithfully, and how to use them to make inferences about the past.

Approaches to historical research vary widely. If you go into the library stacks and browse through any shelf of history books, you will see that even historians who work in narrow geographical and chronological specialties approach their subjects from many different perspectives. They incorporate methods and insights not only from other historians but from scholars in the humanities, the natural sciences, and the social sciences as well. Thus Arthur Ray, in *I Have Lived Here Since the World Began*, draws on geography, literature, anthropology, and economics to recount the history of Canada's First Nations.[5] In fact, the variety of angles from which historians approach their subjects is almost endless.

Despite the diversity of their approaches, however, all historians share a commitment to accurate reporting, persuasive argument, and clear communication—in short, to good writing. *Writing History* is designed to introduce undergraduate historians to the discipline and its challenges by guiding them through the preparation and writing of a research paper (the most common history assignment). Chapter by chapter, it explains the processes of planning, finding a topic, researching, analyzing and incorporating sources, building arguments, and creating a finished work. In addition, Chapter 11 offers a brief guide to various other history writing assignments, including oral history projects, as well as some hints to help with history exams.

This third edition has been extensively revised to enhance its practical value for students and instructors alike. Among its new features is an essay concept map charting all the stages of the research and writing process, designed to help visual learners in particular. While the complete map can be found in the appendix at the end of the book, the relevant portions are repeated at the ends of Chapters 1–4, 6, and 10, to facilitate review of the chapter material. Students will be able to check the map in the appendix as they work through the researching and writing process to ensure that they have not missed any steps and to keep visual track of their progress.

In addition, key terms are now bolded at first use and clearly defined in a glossary at the end of the book, while boxes at the end of each chapter highlight its key points. A handy new Reference Guide inside the front cover tells readers where they can find answers to many frequently asked questions. Finally, inside the back cover are three checklists that students can use to make sure they have covered all the bases before submitting a paper.

᷺ CHAPTER 1 ᷺

GETTING STARTED

CHOOSING A TOPIC

EXPLORE YOUR INTERESTS

When someone at a party asks you what you're interested in, you probably don't stop and reflect: you answer with a quick one-liner. When your history instructor asks you to choose an essay topic, you can take advantage of the opportunity to think about your interests in more depth.

As a student, you may be drawn to the history of medicine because you want to become a doctor; or the history of physics may interest you because you are concerned about nuclear proliferation. Perhaps some historians have sparked your interest through their teaching or writing. When you have the chance to choose your topic, you can use it to explore questions that are significant to you.

MOVE FROM A HISTORICAL INTEREST TO A RESEARCH TOPIC

How do you convert your historical interest into a research topic? First, remembering that your topic must clearly be relevant to the course, look for a small story within your broad range of interests. Think about what it is, specifically, that you enjoy learning about. Let's say that as a child you were fascinated by the stars; as a teenager you read everything you could find about the adventures of eighteenth-century British sea captains like Cook, Bligh, and Vancouver; and last year your favourite course was an introduction to astronomy that touched on the way, before the late eighteenth century, sailors depended on the stars to determine their position at sea. Maybe you could write an essay on the history of navigation?

Unfortunately, this is the sort of topic that is better suited to a massive textbook than to a short essay. Chances are that your time is limited and your teacher has set a page limit for your essay in any case. How can you find a topic that will let you explore your interests but will also accommodate your limitations? Many resources available online or in the library can help you to narrow down your topic.

USING ELECTRONIC RESOURCES

Although history professors usually prefer published sources, the reality is that most students today will begin their research online. There are many worthy online resources, from books and articles to library catalogues and pictures of art and architecture. (See pp. 8–9, "Online Library Resources" and "Sources for Canadian History," for some examples.) But there are also many unworthy sites. The trick is to distinguish between them.

It takes a great deal of time and effort to produce, print, and distribute a book, or even a journal article. Typically, a work of history that is to be published must first be approved not only by a team of editors but by several peer reviewers. Web publishing, on the other hand, is cheap, easy, and free of quality controls. This is why many instructors mistrust online sources and some insist that their students include some traditional books and journal articles, preferably written by recognized specialists in the field. So how do you use online resources wisely?

The best way to find a useful website is to use a high-quality search engine such as Google or the more specialized Google Scholar (http://scholar.google.com/), which gives you access to scholarly and governmental documents and publications. Start with a keyword search. In a keyword search, it's important to use distinctive words. Type in "navigation" and you will get upwards of 800 million entries. The results will be more narrowly focused if you include more terms: for instance, "navigation history Cook". The most useful hits are likely to come near the top of the list, but be sure to look carefully through at least the first few pages. In the course of scanning these entries you may think of additional terms that will allow you to refine your search even further. Search engines don't understand your thought process, so the more specific your search terms are, the more relevant the results will be.

Check the address and sponsor. When you find a promising site, note the address, the author, the title, the owner of the domain, and the date of publication. This will not only help you to evaluate the site, but will allow you to give a proper **citation** later, when you are writing. Beware of sites that are trying to sell you a product or service, or that leave you wondering "who wrote this?" Often the best sites are affiliated with academic, government, or non-profit institutions. At the very least, the content of these sites has been judged acceptable by the sponsoring organizations, and in many cases it will represent the official view. On the subject of navigation, for example, the National Maritime Museum in Greenwich, England, has a highly informative web page on the instruments used for celestial navigation, complete with illustrations, at www.nmm.ac.uk/collections/explore/index.cfm/category/90490/#aboutColl.

By contrast, you should be particularly cautious with web addresses ending in ".com" or ".co": these are commercial sites, and anybody with a credit card can create one. This is not to say that all commercial sites are bad (or that all academic sites are good), but checking the extension is one way to begin sorting through a long list of possible sites.

Has the material on the site been published in print? Many sites begin as print sources, or are published in both print and electronic editions. The quality of these sites is often high, because print media tend to have relatively strict quality controls.

Is the information on the site available elsewhere? There are now some outstanding websites associated with museums and historical archives. In these cases, the actual sources of the information published online are available in physical form. Thus the journals of Sir Joseph Banks, who travelled with Captain Cook and kept detailed records of their observations in Australia, are available online at www.sl.nsw.gov.au/banks/, but can also be found in their original form at the State Library of New South Wales, Australia.

Be skeptical. Some websites are invaluable for historians, some are completely useless, and many are just mediocre. How can you tell the difference? Assess the tone of the writing. Is it scholarly? Or is the author ranting, trying to convert you to some belief or opinion? Does the coverage seem thorough and balanced? Is there a clear point of view? If so, is there significant evidence to substantiate the point of view? Is it consistent with evidence from other sources? Is the evidence used fairly and reasonably? Can it be verified? Are there any obvious factual errors? Is the site presented by scholars whose names and affiliations you recognize and respect? Pay attention as well to the site's organization and writing. Is the organization clear and logical? Can you spot any errors in grammar or punctuation?

When in doubt, ask your professor. None of the criteria listed above are enough on their own to determine a site's reliability, but together they can help. If you still have doubts about a particular site, ask your professor to check it for you, perhaps via e-mail message, containing the Internet address of the website in question. It's always better to ask about a source in advance than to be asked about it after you have turned in the paper.

What about Wikipedia? Wikipedia is a collaborative encyclopedia made up of entries that can be written or edited by anyone with access to a computer. In other words, the material it contains can be modified or changed—added to or subtracted from—and that is where the danger lies. Much of the material on Wikipedia is properly referenced, and much is reliable. However, because there are few quality controls, the reliability is not consistent, and academic opinions on its usefulness differ. You can certainly ask your professor if Wikipedia is an acceptable starting-point for a research project. If it is, looking at the site may give you an initial idea of the scope of your topic, some ideas about areas for research, and perhaps some sources to investigate. But Wikipedia alone cannot serve as the basis for a real research paper, and in any case you will need to verify any material you find there by checking other sources. Since most historians begin their research with published sources, so should you. Now is the time to go to the library.

USING PRINT SOURCES

Visit the reading room of any good library and you will find a collection of reference works—encyclopedias, dictionaries, and textbooks—covering a broad range of interests and topics. (Many encyclopedias and dictionaries are also available online or as CD-ROMS.)

Encyclopedias. A good encyclopedia can give you a broad overview of a topic. It will contain basic explanations as well as hints about related subjects. Just keep in mind that encyclopedia articles can't provide anything more than an introduction. They are not substantial enough to serve as the basis of a paper. Nevertheless, the *Encyclopedia Britannica* does contain a useful 10-page summary of the history of navigation, stretching from the beginnings of marine navigation to the recent development of global positioning satellites. The article includes both general and technical overviews of the basic problems of navigation and their solutions, as well as illustrations and a **bibliography**. In this case, an encyclopedia article could help to jump-start a research project.

Dictionaries. Dictionaries also offer a quick way to explore some topics. There are three different types of dictionary, each of which has its own special uses. *Prescriptive* dictionaries like *Webster's* will tell you how words should be used; *descriptive* dictionaries like the *Canadian Oxford Dictionary* will tell you how words are actually used; and *historical* dictionaries like the *Oxford English Dictionary* will tell you how words have been used over time. Some, such as *The Gage Canadian Dictionary*, include both prescriptive and descriptive features.

In the case of navigation, dictionaries probably have little to offer, but they are still worth a look. The meaning of "navigation" is clear enough, and so are its origins (from the Latin *navis* for ship). You may be interested to find that the *Oxford English Dictionary* identifies eight different shades of meaning for the word "navigation", some dating to the sixteenth century. But this information doesn't raise any interesting research questions.

Textbooks. Some textbooks may contain useful surveys of your topic, and they are sure to contain bibliographies. For information on navigation, more than one type of text could prove to be useful. A textbook on world history or the history of science might include some reference to changes in navigational methods over time. A textbook on astronomy or navigation might provide some helpful technical explanations. Be sure to check textbook bibliographies for further references.

The AHA Guide. Another way to find useful references is to look in The American Historical Association's *Guide to Historical Literature.*[6] Although the most recent edition dates to 1995, it can be a valuable guide to works published before the 1990s. It is organized into common fields of specialization, such as "Canada," "Central Asia," and "International Relations since 1920." Each section begins with a short essay by a specialist, describing the main research problems in the field. A table of contents then lists the subcategories in which the relevant books are organized, beginning with other reference works. In addition to bibliographical information (author, title, and so on), each entry includes a brief summary of the work and an assessment of its value.

The works listed in the bibliography can give a beginning researcher a head start. And each section of the *Guide* begins with that might help you if you cannot find clues within the *Guide.* Almost every broad subject in history has its own special reference works, and these might help you to find more sources.

Suppose you wanted to conduct a search for "navigation" in the AHA *Guide.* The main table of contents indicates that there is a section on "Science, Technology, and Medicine" on page 77. Turn there and the first thing you will find is an essay by Robert Dekosky that provides a broad survey of the main issues in the field. The bibliographical section begins on page 81 with a table of contents listing the categories in which entries are organized. Your first stop should be the reference works. Then you can take a look at several other categories that might be related to navigation: "Modern Astronomy, Cosmology, and Astrophysics," "Scientific Instruments," and "Naval and Maritime Technology."

Each of these categories includes its own list of reference guides. You will see that the editors of the scholarly journals *Isis* and *Technology and Culture* compile annual bibliographies on all subjects relating to the history of science and technology. The bibliographies before 1976 are available in hard copy, and the bibliographies after 1976 are available both in hard copy and on CD-ROM. This is just one example of the information available in the AHA *Guide*. After scanning the reference subheadings, you may find that the sections on "Modern Astronomy, Cosmology, and Astrophysics" and "Naval and Maritime Technology" are not especially useful for your purpose. But the section on "Scientific Instruments" does list a number of interesting titles. Based on what you have found in the AHA *Guide*, you can now track down the most promising works. Don't forget to search the bibliographies from *Isis* and *Technology and Culture* as well.

ASK A LIBRARIAN

By the time you have exhausted your library's main reference collection, you will have accumulated a list of titles. Now you will need to start looking in the library catalogue for the titles of books that are kept in the stacks. If you still don't feel comfortable searching the catalogue, ask a librarian for help. Librarians are the unsung heroes of the historical world. Historians depend heavily on them, because they not only preserve information but know how it is organized, and therefore can help historians find what they need. When in doubt, ask a librarian.

   In the case of navigation, almost any librarian would know that the main bibliographies in the history of science and technology are compiled by *Isis* and *Technology and Culture*. Librarians also know other ways to search for bibliographies and basic reference works.

EXPLORE THE LIBRARY CATALOGUE

Library catalogues can be a tremendous help in the search for works on a particular subject. Most are now computerized and accessible online. However, since library holdings change constantly, it's still a good idea to talk with a librarian—a research specialist—before you begin to search the catalogue. The key to searching a computerized catalogue is understanding how the information is organized. Most items in the library are listed by author, title, and subject heading. In order to find the right headings, start with a keyword search. Again, the choice of words is crucial. "Navigation history Cook" will probably take you to several works, each of which will have subject headings. Click on the subject headings to link to other works on the same subject. Please note that subject searches are different from keyword searches. A keyword search may turn up your terms in many different orders, but subject headings are fixed by the US Library of Congress. You won't hit a subject heading unless you type in its exact wording. (All librarians will be able to explain to you how to search for Library of Congress subject headings.) Once you come across a useful subject heading, follow the links to other headings. Click on author and title links to identify related works.

EXPLORE ONLINE LIBRARY RESOURCES

One advantage of doing an electronic search at the library is that all the resources it makes available will be worthwhile. Talk with your reference librarians about the **databases** available through your institution. You may be able to browse through all of them. If so, think about broad topic areas to check for your particular project: there may be databases not only for history, but also for anthropology, business, politics, and Canadian, Aboriginal, or women's studies. Reference librarians are experts in electronic searches, and most will be happy to show you how to begin.

Libraries subscribe to many different online services. Small college libraries cannot afford all the resources that their counterparts at big research universities can, but several types of service are commonly available. Along with encyclopedias and dictionaries, back issues of historical journals are now sometimes available online. Indexes of articles and unpublished dissertations are also available by library subscription.

Colleges and universities buy access to controlled websites, library portals, and databases so that you can use them for research. Databases typically give you access to online periodicals that you will not find through a Google-type search; you can usually search for particular journals, subjects, authors, topics, and keywords. Once you find useful resources, you can print them or e-mail them to yourself. But you should be aware that computerized indexes may not list articles that were written before the 1980s, and that the indexes themselves may be out of date by a year or two. It pays to check the "hard copy" indexes and tables of contents for titles that are either very old or very new.

A variety of online services will search through multiple databases that used to exist only in print form, such as Books In Print, the Humanities Index, the Social Science Index, and Dissertation Abstracts (a guide to over a million doctoral dissertations from all over the world), although some of these databases allow full access only through libraries that subscribe to the service. Many college libraries subscribe to EBSCO Host, which gives you access to articles from a huge variety of journals. Similarly, JSTOR, "The Scholarly Journal Archive," offers access to back issues of scholarly (mostly American and British) journals in many fields, including history (some of JSTOR's holdings go back as far as the seventeenth century). Libraries purchase subscriptions to specific groups of publications in JSTOR. The same is true of ProQuest, a database that allows you to search for dissertations as well as articles and will eventually provide access to several billion images. The University of Illinois' History Cooperative site provides easy access to full-text journal articles, historical map collections, and historians' web links. Historical Abstracts allows you to find abstracts (summaries of the most important points) of articles and book reviews from more than 2,000 journals from all over the world; for Canadian as well as US history, see under "American History and Life, File 38." Project Muse® (available only through subscribing libraries) carries an online database, searchable by keyword or phrase, of more than 400 journals, including the *Canadian Historical Review* and the *Journal of Canadian Studies*.

Some online search services deliver the full texts of articles. If the full text is not immediately available, the article may be requested through Interlibrary Loan. Some Interlibrary Loan services now deliver articles electronically.

SOURCES FOR CANADIAN HISTORY

A wide variety of reference works and bibliographies on Canadian topics are available in most college and university libraries. Bibliographies list books and articles that focus on particular topics. They may be arranged alphabetically, geographically, or chronologically by subject matter or date of publication, and these categories are often cross-referenced. You can use them to get ideas of titles to search for in your own library, through Interlibrary Loan, or online. General bibliographies include *Canadian History: A Reader's Guide*, *The Oxford Companion to Canadian History and Literature* (and its Supplement), *Introducing Canada: An Annotated Bibliography of Canadian History in English*, and *Canadian Reference Sources: An Annotated Bibliography*.[7] In addition to simple lists of bibliographical sources in various topic areas, many of these works contain articles on places, individuals, groups, political parties, governmental policies, business affairs, and so on.

You might also check to see whether your library has any more general historical bibliographies, such as the Historical Association's *Annual Bulletin of Historical Literature*, which publishes reviews of recent books, journals, and journal articles as well as special sections on specific areas (such as "the Americas") and specific time periods.[8] In addition, university libraries sometimes have bibliographical collections specific to particular regions, which may be worth checking. Depending on your area of research, it may also be useful to check the holdings of municipal and provincial archives, public libraries, and museums.

Once you have a more specific idea of the area you want to research, you might also check for specialized bibliographies. If you were interested in women's history, for example, you could look at *Changing Women, Changing History: A Bibliography of the History of Women in Canada*. For First Nations' history you would want to check references such as *The Ethnographic Bibliography of North America*. For military history, you might consult *The Canadian Military Experience 1867–1995: A Bibliography*. Perhaps you are interested in regional history? In that case you might look for books such as *A Bibliography of British Columbia* or (for even more local content) *The Vancouver Centennial Bibliography*.[9] Similar works exist for many other regions.

Among the general Canadian reference works at your disposal are *The Canadian Encyclopedia* and *The Dictionary of Canadian Biography* (both available online as well as in print), *The Oxford Companion to Canadian History*, the *Encyclopedia of Canada's Peoples*, *Canadian Who's*

Who, the *Canadian Annual Review of Politics and Public Affairs*, and the *Fitzhenry and Whiteside Book of Canadian Facts and Dates.*[10] In many cases the articles in these books contain lists of sources, so be sure to check them for additional ideas. Another important reference work is the *Historical Atlas of Canada*, which has been published in a three-volume set as well as a concise edition, and which includes short articles and bibliographies for most of its maps.[11] Regional or local encyclopedias and atlases can be useful as well, depending on your topic.

Periodicals and scholarly journals can also be valuable sources for Canadian history. Probably the best way to find relevant articles is to search the various periodical indexes. These list articles from journals, magazines, and newspapers, and they are arranged alphabetically both by subject and by author. Most college libraries carry *The Canadian Periodical Index*, *The Canadian Magazine Index*, *The Social Sciences Index*, *The Humanities Index*, and *The Canadian Index*, all of which are reasonably easy to use. *The Canadian Index*, for example, lists citations for articles from several hundred journals, both scholarly and popular, covering a broad range of topic areas. It is particularly useful for biographical information not just on figures such as politicians and military leaders, but on people such as artists and authors, both historical and contemporary. Most indexes allow you to search for keywords as well as specific names or subject areas.

If you find articles in journals that your institution does not carry, you can usually access them online or through Interlibrary Loan. Some historical journals, such as the *Canadian Historical Review*, have their own indexes for ease of research. Be sure to find out whether any specialized journals might offer material relevant to your topic. Journals such as *Urban History Review, Prairie Forum, Newfoundland Studies*, and *Labour/Le Travail* fall into this category.

Finally, a few words about electronic searches and sources. In addition to the online sources outlined above, there are many other sites that deal directly with Canadian historical material. The Library and Archives Canada site, for instance, offers what it calls "the Canadian national catalogue" of the published materials held in more than 1,300 libraries across the country. This is an excellent site for locating specific material. It also offers links to resources such as other federal government sites, the Portrait Gallery of Canada, the online Dictionary of Canadian Biography, the Canadian Genealogy Centre, and an excellent "research tool" called ArchiviaNet that can take you to a number of searchable data and photograph collections. You can find Library and Archives at www.collectionscanada.ca/index_e.html. Another useful resource is Canada in the Making, at www.canadiana.org/citm/index_e.html. Based on the Government Documents section of the Early Canadiana Online collection, it offers narrative texts and links to primary sources, as well as collections of related materials to help you explore themes such as "Aboriginal Treaties" or "Pioneers and Immigrants." The Canadian Institute for Historical Microreproductions offers easy access to early Canadian printed materials at www.canadiana.org/eco.php?doc=cihm. The Our Roots project (www.ourroots.ca), concentrates on Canadian local history materials. Finally, most general textbooks on Canadian history contain lists of publicly available sites that are worth checking.

APPROACH YOUR TOPIC FROM A PARTICULAR ANGLE

A library at a large university may contain hundreds of items on the subject of navigation, and it could also have special collections of manuscripts and artifacts. Even a small library may have several dozen items on navigation. Don't be discouraged. You simply need to bring more focus to your topic.

Think back to the books you have read and the courses you have taken. If you like reading biographies, then you might want to focus on an individual who made a significant contribution to the field. If you prefer social history, you might choose a topic along the lines of class, gender, or race. You might be especially interested in the history of a particular place or time period. Keep working in the reference room until you have identified a reasonably focused topic and a manageable number of resources that you can use as the basis of your research.

Suppose you are still interested in writing about the history of navigation. While searching the library catalogue, you decide to find a biography of Captain Cook. You skim the list, looking for a relevant recent work, and find Brian W. Richardson's *Longitude and Empire: How*

Captain Cook's Voyages Changed the World, published in 2005. Now you have a new term to search for: "longitude".

GO TO THE LIBRARY AND DO SOME BACKGROUND READING

Searching cannot be done exclusively from a computer terminal or a card catalogue. It's time to go to the library stacks. Locate Richardson's book on Captain Cook's voyages and skim the index to find out where it discusses navigation and longitude. You will find an interesting section on pages 34 and 35 on eighteenth-century methods of calculating longitude. Here is a specific problem in the history of navigation: how to use celestial observations and mathematical calculations to determine a position and plot a course. Now you might have a specific topic.

As you define your topic, you will find yourself moving back and forth between the catalogue and the stacks. Go back to the catalogue and search under "longitude." Here, among many items, you notice a promising subheading: "Longitude—Measurement—History." One of the listings looks especially promising: Dava Sobel's *Longitude: The True Story of a Lone Genius Who Solved the Greatest Scientific Problem of His Time* (New York: Walker, 1995) summarizes the scientific problems surrounding longitude, but its main subject is John Harrison, the clockmaker who struggled against great odds to build the first marine chronometer, the essential instrument for calculating longitude. Because it lacks **footnotes**, Sobel's book falls into the category of **popular** rather than **scholarly history** and therefore is not suitable as a source for an academic paper. However, it does contain a short bibliography that could be useful.

Under the same subject heading, you also find a book called *The Quest for Longitude*, edited by William Andrewes, which summarizes the proceedings of a historical conference held at Harvard in 1993. The book contains numerous illustrations and technical discussions, but most important for your present purposes, it also contains a number of scholarly articles on longitude, as well as substantial footnotes and an extensive bibliography. Now you have three sources that can point you in further directions.

BROWSE FOR MORE SOURCES

There is only one way to make an informed choice about a topic: go to the library stacks and browse through the potential source materials. Look for both quantity and quality. Are there enough sources to write this paper, or are there so many that you will have to define your topic more narrowly? It's also important to consider when various sources were published. Are you finding the most recent work in the field? A book that was published decades ago could well be out of date.

In the case of longitude, the Sobel, Andrewes, and Richardson books can all be used as guides to additional sources. All three were published relatively recently, and all contain fairly comprehensive bibliographies. It's usually a good idea to start with a narrow base of sources and build it into a broader base. Therefore, try to find some of the sources in Sobel's short bibliography, and as you dig more deeply, draw on the longer lists provided by Andrewes and Richardson. As you search through the stacks, you will find more clues that will lead you to further sources. If you look at the shelves where your specific sources are stored, you may also find other books on similar themes. Just keep in mind that there are limits both to your time and to the length of your paper. You don't need to locate every potential source right now: just enough to get you started.

DISTINGUISH PRIMARY SOURCES FROM SECONDARY WORKS

Not all sources are created equal. In particular, historians distinguish between primary and secondary sources.

Primary sources. A **primary source** is one that originates in the time period under study. Such sources take many forms, and not all of them are documents: as well as personal memoirs and correspondence, government or church documents, and transcripts of legal proceedings, they may include oral histories and traditions, archaeological and biological evidence, and visual materials such as sculptures, paintings, and photographs. Primary sources, particularly documents, are the foundations of nearly all historians' work, and your professor may instruct you to use them as well.

Each kind of primary source must be considered on its own terms. Historians used to think that materials such as government documents were inherently more reliable than others. But even government documents are not entirely straightforward or objective. Like all sources, they reveal some things and obscure others. This means that you need to think carefully not just about the author and purpose of every document, but about its intended audience. Why was the document produced, and what effect was it supposed to have? What does it tell you about the time, the place, the people?

Secondary sources. Typically, a **secondary source** is a book or article that reflects on and interprets a primary source. Secondary works range from scholarly works by professional historians to journalistic accounts. Just as we are shaped by our environments and the events of our own times, so secondary works vary depending on the place and time in which they were written. For example, the growth of activist feminism in the later 1960s and the 1970s led to an expansion of women's history, and, more recently, some important land claims disputes have refocused historians' attention on Canada's Aboriginal peoples. Every secondary work must be evaluated on its own merits, particularly on how well it uses primary sources as evidence; but as a general rule, you should always look for the most up-to-date work you can find. In some cases the distinction between primary sources and secondary works may be confusing. If you are writing about historical writers, for instance, you may find yourself using a secondary work as a primary source. In the 1880s and 1890s, for example, an English-born Canadian named William Kingsford wrote a 10-volume *History of Canada* that celebrated the new Dominion as the triumph of British values. Since it tells us as much about the attitudes of middle-class anglophones in Kingsford's day as it does about the events leading up to Confederation, Kingsford's work could be used as a primary source for a study of Canada in the late nineteenth century.

DISTINGISH SCHOLARLY FROM POPULAR HISTORY

Not everyone who writes history is a trained historian. Professional historians and history professors undergo many years of study as well as rigorous training in the standards of evidence and accuracy. How can you tell a scholarly source from popular history?

Scholarly history. Scholarly books have gone through rigorous editing and **peer review** (check the acknowledgements page to see whether reviewers are mentioned) and often assume that their readers will have some background in the field. Most scholarly history is based on original research and is designed to inform rather than entertain. There will be plenty of footnotes, so that you can evaluate their evidence for yourself if you wish, and a full, detailed bibliography. Unless the subject is art history, such works typically have few, if any, illustrations or photographs. Look also particularly for books published by university or other presses that concentrate on academic work (for confirmation, check the publisher's website). The Andrewes book mentioned above is an example of a scholarly source.

Historians also write scholarly articles, sometimes in the preliminary stages of research for an eventual book and sometimes simply on topics that interest them. One advantage of articles for students is that they are short. More important, though, an article can usually be researched, written, and published far more quickly than a book: therefore articles tend to reflect both the latest thinking on a given subject and the most current methodology. For example, devastating windstorms in 2006 and 2007 that destroyed much of Vancouver's Stanley Park inspired the historian Sean Kheraj to find out more about the history of the park. The result was his article "Restoring Nature: Ecology, Memory and the Storm History of Vancouver's Stanley Park", published in the December 2007 edition of the *Canadian Historical Review*.

Look for articles in journals published either by academic institutions or by organizations such as the Champlain Society (which is devoted to preserving Canada's documentary heritage) or the Canadian Historical Association. These journals generally list an editorial board made up mainly of academics, and refer articles to peer reviewers before accepting them for publication. They contain little or no advertising and are usually published quarterly. You will usually find these journals only in libraries, particularly academic libraries, and you will often find back issues shelved together in annual bound volumes. *The Canadian Historical Review, BC Studies,* and *Past and Present* are all examples of scholarly periodicals.

Popular history. In contrast, history written by people not specifically trained in history, such as journalists, is generally classified as popular. Such books often contain many photographs and they are designed to interest, or even entertain, non-scholarly readers as much as to inform them. They are not likely to have undergone peer review, and they generally do not include many references. The Sobel book, with its brief bibliography, is typical.

The magazines you see on newsstands are usually non-scholarly. They typically have striking colour pictures on the front cover, are produced on glossy paper, and contain a lot of advertising and photographs. They are usually published weekly or monthly, their articles may be anonymous or written by staff reporters, and they will rarely have references or bibliographies. *Maclean's* is a typical popular magazine.

None of this is to say that all academic history is excellent and all popular history is second-rate. It is also only fair to point out that some academic historians also publish popular history and that some "amateur" historians produce work of very high quality. For example, Professor H.V. Nelles, who is a well-known academic historian, wrote *A Little History of Canada*[12] specifically for non-specialists, and Heather Robertson, a professional writer who did not train as a historian, recently published *Measuring Mother Earth*, an interesting account of Joseph Burr Tyrell, the nineteenth-century surveyor, explorer, and adventurer who discovered the first dinosaur skull in Canada.[13] Some newsstand magazines straddle the line between popular and academic: *Canada's History* (formerly known as *The Beaver*), *History Today,* and *Archaeology* often publish articles written by professional historians. So do exercise your judgment when assessing sources, and don't automatically discount popular history. Just check with your professor whenever you aren't sure about the suitability of your source.

FORM A HYPOTHESIS

Naturally, the goal of any researcher is to discover something new. This is a challenging proposition for a student, and by now you may be doubting your choice of topic. Sobel and her predecessors have already written plenty about longitude. What new perspective can you bring to bear on the subject?

One of the most important steps in writing a research paper is to form a **hypothesis**: a question or proposition that will serve as a guide as you work your way through your source materials. As you read through the sources you will look for answers to your question, and as you find more answers you will gradually refine your hypothesis. Over the course of the research process, you will find that you are getting closer to forming an **argument**.

How do you arrive at a hypothesis? One way to begin is to jot down some questions. For example: (1) What sort of person was Harrison? (2) What distinguished Harrison's approach to the problem from that of his competitors? (3) How serious was the problem of finding longitude? (4) Why did the king have to intervene in order for Harrison to receive the recognition he deserved from others in the field?

Now ask yourself two questions. First, if you are able to arrive at an answer to one of those questions, can you build an argument around it? Second, does the question address some broader issue in history? Questions 1 and 3 might yield only descriptions, not arguments. Question 2 could produce a debate (yes, longitude was a serious problem; no, it wasn't so serious), but it would be of little interest to historians today. Question 4 seems a bit more promising. Why did the scientific establishment not recognize the value of Harrison's work? Were the judges responsible for awarding the Longitude Prize influenced by something other than the practical merits of his inventions? The answers to these questions could lead you to ask some broader questions about the social and cultural dimensions of scientific research—a topic of considerable interest to many historians.

DRAFT A PROPOSAL

After you have completed your preliminary research, draft a short proposal. Your teachers and friends may be willing to read it and comment on it. Even if they aren't, the process of writing the proposal will still help you to sketch out your ideas. The proposal is an early opportunity to think critically about your topic.

Every proposal should answer these questions:

1.   What is your topic area? Describe it briefly.
2.   What is the hypothesis that will drive your research?
3.   What will your readers learn from this project? Will you be bringing new information to light, or interpreting common-place knowledge in a new way?
4.   Why is your project significant or interesting? Discuss the relationship between your project and some broader issue in history.
5.   What are your principal sources? Give a short bibliography.
6.   What are your source materials? Will you be relying on library books? Exploring **archival materials**? Analyzing objects or paintings? What methods will you use? Are any of your sources in a foreign or specialized technical language? If so, can you understand them? Will you be using methods from another discipline, such as sociology?

WRITE AN ANNOTATED BIBLIOGRAPHY

The next step is to compile an **annotated bibliography**. This exercise will help you assess the breadth and significance of the sources you have found. List your references according to the instructions for creating a bibliography in Chapter 5 below. Now, after each entry, briefly describe the work and explain how you will be using it in your paper. Describe any special circumstances surrounding the source. For example, is it an eyewitness account? Might its author have a specific bias or some particular technical expertise? In general, these remarks should be concise, but you may say more about some sources than others.

An annotated bibliography on longitude might contain the following entries:

Quill, Humphrey. *John Harrison, the Man Who Found Longitude.* London: Baker, 1966. A biography of the eighteenth-century English clockmaker who built the first marine chronometer, solving the problem of how to calculate longitude. Quill respects Harrison's achievements but also criticizes his irascible behaviour, particularly in his interactions with professional astronomers.

Raymo, Chet. *Walking Zero: Discovering Cosmic Space and Time Along the Prime Meridian.* New York: Walker, 2006. Raymo is a professor emeritus of physics and astronomy and his discussion of Harrison focuses mainly on placing his inventions in the context of other scientific discoveries. He portrays the man himself as an obsessed perfectionist, but describes the fourth clock as an "artifact of Harrison's genius" (151).

Richardson, Brian W. *Longitude and Empire: How Captain Cook's Voyages Changed the World.* Vancouver: University of British Columbia Press, 2005. A wide-ranging book that discusses not only Cook's voyages themselves, but also how they pulled the world together into an integrated whole and helped pave the way physically and psychologically for the British Empire, not only in a political sense, but also in a moral sense.

Sobel, Dava. *Longitude: The True Story of a Lone Genius Who Solved the Greatest Scientific Problem of His Time.* New York: Walker & Co., 1995. A popular biography. Sobel presents Harrison as a hero who triumphed in the face of unreasonable opposition from professional astronomers. No reference notes included.

Notice that the Raymo entry includes a direct quotation, with the specific page reference. Always be sure to record the source of any direct quotation: doing this as you go along will save you many tedious hours checking sources later.

TALK ABOUT YOUR TOPIC

Don't be bashful. Talk about your topic with other people: friends, relatives, teachers, even specialists in the field. If you were researching longitude, for instance, you might seek out a specialist in geography or astronomy, or try to find some navigational equipment and ask an expert to show you how to use it. Experts are usually happy to discuss specific research questions, especially if the questions are thoughtful. If the experts happen to teach at your university, you may be able to visit them during their office hours; if not, make appointments to see them and consider submitting your question(s) in writing, some time in advance.

IF YOU HAVE TO ABANDON A TOPIC, DO IT EARLY

Finding sources, forming a hypothesis, and drafting a proposal will test the viability of your project. It's possible that, at the end of that process, you will decide that you haven't found enough sources, or that the topic is less interesting than you had expected, or that your research has led you to a different, more promising topic area. If the project isn't working, it's better to bail out of it early than to go down in flames later. But you will need time to start over. Of course, this means that you should begin working on any project as soon as possible.

✎ REVIEW ✎
1. Find a topic that interests you.
2. Mine your library for print and online sources.
3. Read bibliographies to find more sources.
4. Make sure your sources are appropriate.
5. Read to develop a hypothesis and craft a proposal.

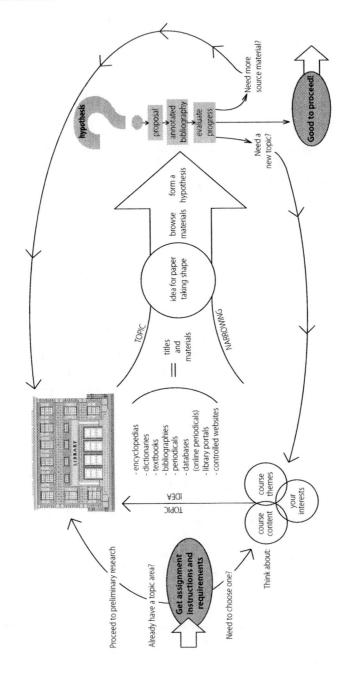

CHAPTER 2

INTERPRETING SOURCE MATERIALS

At first you may find that your sources seem confusing or even contradictory. An important part of writing history is deciding how to interpret and assemble material from sources that may raise more questions than they answer. Some sources will lead historians on an exhilarating chase that culminates in a dead end. Others will make it possible to recover unexpected tales from the past. Fortunately, there are many ways of interpreting source materials.

WORK SYSTEMATICALLY

Historians do not make random choices. They work as systematically as possible, selecting their evidence according to rules that they share with writers across the disciplines. Hippocrates' advice to ancient Greek doctors might well apply to today's historians:

> In Medicine one must pay attention not to plausible theorizing but to experience and reason together. . . . I agree that theorizing is to be approved, provided that it is based on facts, and systematically makes its deductions from what is observed. . . . But conclusions drawn by the unaided reason can hardly be serviceable; only those drawn from observed facts.[14]

Some of these fundamental notions have been debated for thousands of years. What is "plausible theorizing"? Is the difference between reason and irrationality simply a matter of objective systematization? Or does reason have to be subjectively "approved", "observed", and "aided" by people? Historians have often explored questions like these in their efforts to understand how to write history.

WHO? WHAT? WHY? WHERE? WHEN?

Richard Marius is a historian who began his career as a journalist. In his *Short Guide to Writing about History*, he advises students to approach source materials the same way reporters approach stories: by asking five basic questions.[15] It's good advice.

Suppose that you're writing an essay on Louis Riel and your sources consist mainly of nineteenth-century archival materials. Your hypothesis questions whether Riel's militancy represented the majority political view on the South Saskatchewan River in 1884–5. As you read about Riel's decisions, consider organizing your research around the reporter's questions. When you start to get answers, take notes and use them to help you develop ideas for your essay.

"Who" questions. Historians ask "who" to learn biographical information about significant actors, to find out who caused things to happen and who bore the brunt of historical changes. In the case of Riel, you could use "who" questions to acquaint yourself with the various characters involved. What groups made up the South Saskatchewan community? Who actively supported Riel? Who actively opposed him? Who remained on the fringes?

"What" questions. Different sources often describe the same events differently. Know each version of events so that you can compare accounts. Suppose you are focusing on Riel's decision to return to the North-West in 1884. What did he understand of the situation there after living in the US for some years? What did he know of the population and the wider political realities? What did he do to find out about the situation? What did he do to gain support for his decisions and actions? What were the strategic and political consequences of his return?

"Why" questions. Why did some things change while others remained the same? Using each source, make a list of possible causes of events. Try to distinguish the most significant causes from the background causes. Why was Riel successful in his 1870 rebellion but not in 1885? Did the answer lie in himself, in others, or in the changed circumstances? Was

his leadership less effective in 1885? Had he himself changed? Was the level or the quality of community different? Was the response from the federal government different?

"Where" questions. In some cases you will find fairly self-evident answers to "where" questions. In others geographical considerations will open your eyes to unexpected circumstances. You might even find it helpful to draw a map of your subject. Where, for example, is Batoche? Was this a wise choice for his headquarters? Might a stronger stand have been made elsewhere? Might a different location have affected the level or quality of the support he received? What was the route of the new railway? Did this route make a difference to the outcome of events?

"When" questions. Historians analyze change and continuity over time. Not surprisingly, it's important to know when historical events happened. Depending on the topic, you may get an easy answer, a complex one, or no answer at all. Do your best to determine when things happened. Then use this information to place events in a chronological relationship. Try to make one timeline from all your source materials so that you can see the order of events. When, for example, did Riel decide to move from petitions and diplomatic appeals to armed resistance? If he had made this decision earlier, might the outcome have been different? Would the federal government have been able to send troops just as quickly?

"How" questions. Marius did not include "how" questions in his list, but they are also helpful to think about. In the case of Riel, you might want to ask how events played out and how they fit into a wider context. How did Riel and local Métis leaders relate to one another? How did the press in Ontario and Quebec react to the news of the events on the South Saskatchewan? How were political decisions and actions affected by Riel's activities? How did the arrival of the railway influence the decisions of the politicians? How did the Riel affair affect the delicate balance between Ontario and Quebec? How did it affect the development of Quebec nationalism?

BE SENSITIVE TO POINTS OF VIEW

As you use your hypothesis to work through the source materials, you will come to see that many sources present history from a particular point of view. Even photographs show only the perspective of the photographer. Photographers have been known to pose or arrange their subjects, and the mere presence of a camera often changes the way people behave. How do you know which sources to trust? Historians must be sensitive to the fact that those who record events as they happen are likely to describe only the events they consider interesting or important.

Similarly, participants are likely to describe events from their own point of view. In her article "To See Ourselves as the Other's Other: Nlaka'pamux Contact Narratives", Wendy Wickwire discusses the explorer Simon Fraser's encounters with the Nlaka'pamux people of south-central British Columbia. Using both Fraser's journal (the more widely known historical source) and Nlaka'pamux oral history, Wickwire finds many similarities between the two accounts, but also some differences. One of the most striking differences concerns Fraser's encounter with a young woman, an encounter that is not mentioned in the diary but is presented as a highly significant event in the oral account. In this case, each account focused on the concerns of the participants and was created from that perspective alone. A similar point can be made about all contemporary sources: a chronicler's decisions on what to record generally reflect a combination of personal and community perspectives on what is important and what is not—or, sometimes, what one ought to keep silent about.[16]

The creation of source materials does not end with the choices made by the chroniclers. All sorts of factors determine whether or not a chronicle will survive and be accessible. Sometimes records are destroyed by fire, flood, or war. Often collectors, archivists, and librarians decide to preserve some records and discard others. They have their own visions of the past, and politics and economics can influence their decisions in many ways.

During the 1960s, a distinguished historian of science named Loren Graham began to collect information about a Soviet engineer named Peter Palchinsky, who was executed by Stalin in 1929. Graham believed that Palchinsky had made significant contributions to early Soviet engineering, but that the Soviet government was hiding his papers because he had criticized the regime. Graham had to wait almost thirty years, but he finally gained access to Palchinsky's papers after the collapse of the Soviet Union. Then, in a nice twist of fate, he found that the Palchinsky papers shed light on the failure of the Soviet system. His quest for sources became a subplot of his history, *The Ghost of the Executed Engineer.*[17] But even in Graham's case, the choices made by the chroniclers influenced the writing of history.

SELECT THE MOST IMPORTANT INFORMATION

If you want to make an argument, it's not enough just to collect facts; you have to select the relevant ones and arrange them in a suitable structure. You can't include everything in your essay. You must choose the information you need to make your point, even if that means ignoring some interesting tangents or anecdotes.

In the course of your research, you will find some information that is directly relevant to your essay and much that is not. Don't feel bad if you've spent a lot of time investigating a source, only to find that it doesn't contribute to your essay's main idea. If you are tempted to include such material anyway, just to show your readers how hard you have worked, resist the temptation. Readers will be much more impressed by a coherent essay in which all the content is clearly relevant to the main point.

TAKE NOTES SELECTIVELY

You should start taking notes as soon as you begin to analyze your sources. Some historians use notebooks or index cards; others use word-processing or database programs. The method you choose will depend in part on the type of research you are conducting and in part on your personal preference. As you do more research, you will get a better sense of how you like to work.

Much more important than the way you take notes is what they contain. In most cases you don't want to copy your sources word for word. You want to write down only the information that is likely to be useful in your essay. But how do you know what is going to be useful before you begin to write? Making these decisions is the most difficult part of note-taking. You don't want to write down useless information, but you recognize that some irrelevant-looking information may turn out to be useful later on.

It's difficult to know in advance which notes will be useful. This is why you should use your hypothesis to help you read sources. Ask yourself how each source relates to your hypothesis, and jot down notes from the source that answer fundamental questions about your hypothesis. Use your hypothesis to help select the most important information from your sources.

The trickiest thing at this stage is that your hypothesis is likely to change. This is as it should be. Over the course of your research, as you learn more about your subject, your ideas about it will become clearer and you will be able to refine your hypothesis to the point where it can become a **thesis** or argument. Unfortunately, this means that your early notes will be more extensive and less useful than your later notes. Don't be disappointed if, at the end of a project, you find that you've taken some notes that you didn't need: this is a natural consequence of the process of selection and refinement.

✐ REVIEW ✐

1. *Think* as you read.
2. Question your sources.
3. Be aware of sources' points of view.
4. Take notes that are relevant to your hypothesis.

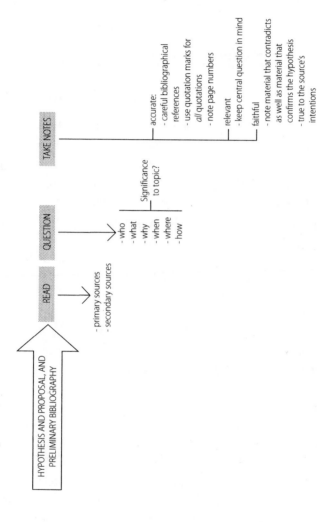

CHAPTER 3

USING SOURCES

It is impossible to know exactly what happened in the past, but that has not stopped people from writing about it. The American poet Walt Whitman (1819–92) wrote that the "interior history" of his country's Civil War "will not only never be written—its practicality, minutiae of deeds and passions, will never be even suggested."[18] That may be true, but it did not stop Whitman from trying to interpret the war by making reasoned inferences from sources.

An **inference** is more than a hunch. It is an intelligent conclusion reached through examination and comparison of evidence. After visiting a number of wounded soldiers in an army hospital, Whitman concluded that the war was indescribably brutal. When he put his conclusion in writing, people believed him even though he had not seen every casualty or every battlefield. He had seen enough wounded men to build his inference into a persuasive argument. Like Whitman, historians arrive at probable interpretations by using their sources to make inferences.

What is it that makes an inferential argument interesting? Good writers make inferences by juxtaposing sources in a new, provocative way. At a time when people on both sides, North and South, were mobilizing armies to kill and maim one another, Whitman recognized that it would take more than pacifist principles to turn public opinion against the war. It would take evidence, built by inferences into an argument, to change the way that people thought. New evidence, or a new approach to old evidence, called into question the received wisdom of the day.

Inferential reasoning is based on thoughtful comparison. When modern-day historians write about the past, they try never to rely on a single source: they cross-check the information provided by various sources. Even when there is only one source on a given subject, they will assess it in the light of their own general knowledge, look for points of comparison with other works, and use those works to put their material into a wider context.

ABOUT FACTS

Every inference begins with careful consideration of the facts. Determining what the facts are is a large part of a historian's job, of course. But there is no need to start back at square one every time: many facts are easy to recognize and should be taken as given.

Occasionally you may encounter people who are overly skeptical about recognized facts. For example, some people deny that the Holocaust ever happened, despite the millions who experienced, witnessed, and documented it. One organization of polemicists posing as historians even has its own journal dedicated to "proving" its point.[19] Real historical writers investigate factual uncertainties, but they do not invent convenient facts and they don't ignore inconvenient ones. People are entitled to their own opinions—not to their own facts.

TRANSFORM FACTS INTO EVIDENCE

There is more to writing history than simply gathering facts and arranging them in some sort of order. In itself, the existence of a fact doesn't prove anything. Facts gain meaning only when we examine and interpret them. As Professor John H. Arnold remarks, historians try to create

> an interesting, coherent and useful narrative about the past. The past itself is not a narrative. In its entirety, it is as chaotic, uncoordinated, and complex as life. History is about making sense of that mess, finding or creating patterns and meanings and stories from the maelstrom.[20]

Historians seek out the most reliable information and do their best to establish its accuracy before they use it to make inferences.

CHECK YOUR FACTS

It's not always easy to tell where "the facts" stop and the interpretation begins. In Canada, for instance, the 1990s were a period of intense debate on the rights of First Nations. The historical geographer Cole Harris, recognizing that the size of pre-contact indigenous populations in British Columbia could have some bearing on issues such as land claims, also recognized that both Aboriginal and non-Aboriginal estimates could be influenced by political and economic considerations. Therefore he set to determine accurate figures. He did not simply accept the claims of either "side," and he did not accept that it was impossible so many years later to determine the population size. Instead, Harris gathered all the data he could find, examining the oral history traditions of the peoples concerned as well as the written accounts of Europeans and the work of earlier ethnographers. Harris published his research in the first chapter of *The Resettlement of British Columbia*. He concluded that the pre-contact population was probably over 200,000, possibly over 400,000, and that it had been decimated by "European" diseases even before direct contact with Europeans.[21] Follow Cole Harris's example and take an informed but pragmatic approach to facts. Very often, facts will be self-evident, but sometimes historians find that supposed facts rest on nothing more than assumptions and preconceptions. There are several procedures that can help in determining the truth of questionable "facts."

CHECK THE INTERNAL CONSISTENCY OF PRIMARY SOURCES

If a document contradicts itself, there is probably a discernible reason. For example, the richest sources of information on rural north China during the Japanese occupation are the reports written between 1940 and 1942 by teams of sociologists who were sent by the Japanese government's South Manchurian Railway Company to interview large numbers of peasants. These reports contain many contradictions, for the peasants (not surprisingly) mistrusted the occupiers and sometimes lied to them.

Nevertheless, several historians have used the interviews as sources of information on the economy, society, and politics of the region.[22] They have done so using internal inferences—obtained by comparing the statements of individual peasants on specific issues—and then checking them against other sources of information on rural north China.

All sources have been subject to some biases in creation and selection, but that does not mean that historians cannot try to determine what happened.

CHECK PRIMARY SOURCES AGAINST ONE ANOTHER

Comparing source materials can lead to important new inferences. One such breakthrough involved the well-known life of Louis Pasteur, who made some of the most significant contributions to nineteenth-century biology. After Pasteur died in 1895, the accounts of his life published by colleagues and family were uniformly admiring.

Historians knew that they should be skeptical of such sources, but they had no evidence to the contrary until 1938, when Pasteur's nephew and laboratory assistant, Adrien Loir, claimed that the great doctor had misled the judges at the public trials of his anthrax vaccine. Because historians had no evidence to substantiate Loir's claim, however, the heroic myth remained in place until the 1970s, when Pasteur's laboratory notebooks passed out of his family to the French state. When the historian Gerald Geison gained access to them, he found that they confirmed Loir's account. Using the notebooks to re-evaluate Pasteur's experimental practices, Geison moved Loir's account from the background to the foreground and wrote an important book entitled *The Private Science of Louis Pasteur.*[23]

COMPARE PRIMARY AND SECONDARY SOURCES

Historical knowledge changes incrementally as new information alters historians' understanding of the past. When new materials or methods become available, historians often find themselves using primary sources to refine or contradict the ideas proposed by earlier secondary works. One recent example comes from the field of environmental history.

In the West African country of Guinea, the area around the city of Kissidougou is predominantly grassland, with numerous patches of forest. From the 1890s until the 1990s, European scientists visiting the area believed that the patches of trees were remnants of forest that the local inhabitants were converting to grassland. It was only in the 1990s that James Fairhead and Melissa Leach took the trouble to interview the local people and ask them to explain the patches of trees. They were surprised to learn that, contrary to the assumptions of earlier visitors, the villagers had been planting the trees.

Examining a previously unrecognized primary source—the villagers themselves—forced a fundamental reconsideration of the "facts" taken for granted by the secondary European sources. In their book *Misreading the African Landscape*, Fairhead and Leach demonstrated what every good historical writer knows: that historians must cast a skeptical eye on their sources.[24]

Fairhead and Leach uncovered a primary source (oral accounts) that called into question a secondary work, but the reverse is possible, too. A historian named Jan Vansina was able to use his knowledge of a familiar body of secondary works to interpret some unfamiliar primary sources. In 1953, Vansina was visiting the Congo for the first time. He had been studying historical literature on medieval Europe and had written his master's thesis on Latin funerary dirges, but he knew very little about African history (a subject that few Europeans studied in those days). Vansina met a Kuba village historian named Mbop Louis who told him, "We too know the past, because we carry our newspapers in our heads." Mbop recited a historical poem, which reminded Vansina of one of the Latin dirges he knew so well. He realized that the techniques used to interpret medieval European material could be applied to this oral primary source.[25] Vansina went on to write some of the pioneering works in African history.

JUXTAPOSE SOURCES

In the course of your research and writing, you will need to check both primary and secondary sources for internal consistency. You will also need to compare primary sources and secondary works against one another. How does the process of comparison work in practice?

In the 1970s, the historian Robin Fisher studied the effects of contact with Europeans on the First Nations of the Pacific coast. Up to that point, historians had taken little notice of the indigenous peoples of the region that would become British Columbia, but the general view was that their societies had been devastated by the arrival of Europeans on the coast in the late 1700s. Fisher looked at the work of earlier historians and anthropologists. He also read carefully the records and diaries of Spanish, American, and British explorers and traders such as Juan Pérez, Robert Haswell, and James Cook.

Comparing these documents, he found that the First Nations' part in the maritime fur trade had been ignored, and that the effect of the trade on their societies had been misunderstood, in part because of scholars' preconceptions and assumptions. In his seminal book *Contact and Conflict*, Fisher concluded that the peoples of the Pacific coast were sophisticated traders who knew very well how to get what they wanted and were able to set the terms of trade with the Europeans.[26] According to Fisher, the devastation of Native societies came later, as a result of White settlement. Not all historians and anthropologists accepted Fisher's argument, but by using a variety of sources, looking at them with new eyes, and drawing his own conclusions, Fisher sparked an interest in the history of British Columbian Aboriginal peoples that continues to the present.

MOVE FROM INFERENCES TO ARGUMENTS

Making inferences allows historians to say something new. This can be an intimidating proposition, especially if you are a beginning student or working on a topic that has already been studied by many scholars. But judging by the contents of most bookstores, historians are always finding something new to say about old topics. Just when you think the Second World War has been studied to death, a new book appears.

There are many ways to say something new. Experienced historians know that new ideas come out of close and careful comparisons of primary and secondary sources. A new idea in one field can shed light

❧ MAKE INFERENCES FROM MATERIAL SOURCES ❧

Most of the source materials used by academic writers are written documents. However, historians of science and technology, archaeologists, and art historians, among others, frequently analyze material objects. Learning to analyze objects can give you new perspectives, but it takes practice. Among the most common methods used by writers across the disciplines to analyze material evidence are the following (based on an article by Jules Prown called "Mind in Matter"):

1. **Describe the object.** What can you observe about the object itself? Give a physical description. How is the object shaped? If you can measure it, what are its dimensions (size, weight)? If you can't measure it, estimate the dimensions. Can you see any obvious symbols on the object, such as markings, decorations, or inscriptions?

2. **Think about the object.** At this very moment, what is it like to interact with the object? What does the object feel like? When you use it, do you have to take into account its size, weight, or shape? What does the object do, and how? Does it work well? What is it like to use it? How do you feel about using this object? Do you like it? Does it frustrate you? Is it puzzling?

3. **Make an argument about the object.** Can you analyze the object imaginatively and plausibly? Review your descriptions and **deductions**. What sorts of hypotheses can you propose about the object? Can you make a historically significant argument about it? What might it have been like for someone to use this object in the past? Use other sources as a lens for interpreting the object. What other evidence can you use to test your hypotheses, speculations, and deductions?[27]

on an old source; the discovery of a new source can inspire historians to rethink some old ideas. In fact, every historian brings a unique personal perspective to all sources.

Still, novelty for its own sake is pointless. Small inferences must be built into larger arguments, and arguments must be made persuasively. As you read your sources, start thinking about ways to construct your essay. How can you move from asking questions about events and sources to composing a story and developing an argument of your own? This is the most challenging aspect to writing any history. You must consider the arguments of your primary sources and secondary works, then engage them constructively and responsibly.

MAKE REASONABLE INFERENCES FROM YOUR SOURCES

Source materials impose healthy constraints on historical writers. You may have a hunch that English maritime explorers landed in North America before the time of Christopher Columbus, but after careful review of primary sources and secondary works, you will find no evidence to support your hypothesis. Don't worry. You thought that you could make a breathtakingly novel argument, but it is much more important that you recognize the limits of your sources. Don't expect too much from your sources, and don't read into them what you hope to find. Sometimes you may even be able to write an essay about how little you can learn from the sources on a particular subject. Even so, if you cannot use a source to support your argument, you must be prepared to either redefine your questions or move on to another set of sources.

MAKE INFERENCES THAT ARE WARRANTED

How do historians know a good inference from a bad one? Under what circumstances are inferences warranted?

The ancient Greeks divided arguments from inferences into two categories: deduction and **induction**. When you are reading and writing history, use the categories of deduction and induction to help you decide which arguments from inferences are warranted.

Deductive reasoning. In deductive reasoning, a writer makes an inference based on a limited amount of evidence, but the inference is trustworthy because it is consistent with conventional wisdom. In other words, deduction means applying general rules to particular circumstances.

Here is an example of a historical deduction: "The gaps in the Watergate tapes must mean that (US President Richard) Nixon had something to hide." What sort of evidence do historians have to support this statement? The Watergate tapes do contain large gaps, but Nixon never admitted to hiding anything. The White House blamed the gaps on the president's secretary, saying that she had accidentally erased portions of the tapes. Why did most people not believe this? Common sense indicated that the missing passages had contained evidence that would incriminate Nixon; that he had a motive for erasing them; and that he also had the access necessary to do so.

Break this argument down into its deductive components and this is what it looks like:

- Evidence: The Watergate tapes contain large gaps.
- Common-sense warrant: The official explanation is less credible than the idea that the tapes were erased to destroy evidence against the President.
- Inference: The fact that the tapes delivered to investigators were incomplete means that Nixon was hiding something.

Although writers rarely state their reasoning in such a schematic way, common-sense deductions often provide warrants for inferences based on limited information.

On the other hand, common sense can be deceptive. It is possible to challenge the inferences of historical writers by testing whether their warrants really are based on common sense. All historians have heard the story about how Columbus wanted to prove that the Earth was round and not flat. According to the legend, Columbus's contemporaries believed the Earth was flat because they had a weak common-sense warrant:

- Evidence: The Earth appears to be flat.
- Common-sense warrant: Humans can distinguish between flat objects and round objects.
- Inference: The Earth is flat, not round.

In fact, humans can't always distinguish flat objects from round objects, at least not on the planetary scale. If your common-sense warrant is weak, then there must be a flaw in your reasoning. Take care to test your warrants, especially if they are unstated. If you don't test them yourself, your readers certainly will.

Inductive reasoning. Inductive reasoning is often associated with science. This is because inductive reasoning begins with many pieces of evidence and generalizes from them. Induction operates on the warrant that a conclusion based on a large quantity of data is likely to be correct. Take the following statement: "Statistics Canada data suggest that between 1973 and 1998 wealth in Canada was increasingly concentrated in the hands of the rich." What are the components of this inductive statement?

- Evidence: Statistics Canada data show that the gap between the incomes of the richest and poorest families in Canada widened considerably between 1973 and 1998.
- Inductive warrant: If you have plenty of data pointing to the same conclusion, that conclusion is likely correct.
- Inference: Based on the evidence, Canadian wealth was increasingly concentrated in the hands of the rich.

The most common way to test such an inference is to question whether the evidence is sufficient. The underlying inductive warrant is difficult to challenge.

AVOID UNWARRANTED COMPARISONS

To write history is to speak on behalf of people who lived in the past. This is a tremendous responsibility, and it is the reason historians are cautious about comparisons. Some comparisons allow historians to make strong inferences about the past; others are pointless or even irresponsible. In a study of the conflict among German historians over how Nazism and the Holocaust should be interpreted, Charles Maier makes the point that some historical comparisons are "licit" and some are not. He criticizes those historians who compare the Holocaust to other genocides for the inappropriate purpose of alleviating German guilt.[28]

An interesting comparison can be found in John Mack Farragher's account of the British expulsion of the Acadians from their colonial territories in the 1750s. Farragher suggests that this action "was the first episode of state-sponsored ethnic cleansing in North American history."[29] To make the comparison, Farragher juxtaposes the expulsion of the Acadians with twentieth-century episodes of forced migration or ethnic cleansing and demonstrates that the events in Acadia matched the 1992 UN Commission of Experts' definition of the latter. Although the term "ethnic cleansing" was unknown in the eighteenth century, Farragher establishes that the expulsion was comparable to modern events both in its purpose and in its consequences for the Acadians.

AVOID ANACHRONISTIC INFERENCES

Although modern-day comparisons can shed valuable light on historical events, you should never place your subjects in situations that they would not recognize.

Some anachronisms are easy to avoid. No one would suggest Caesar glanced at his wristwatch before crossing the Rubicon. Other types of anachronism may not be so obvious, however. For example, the French historian Georges Lefebvre wanted to use Marxist theory to explain the origins of the French Revolution. But when Lefebvre wrote his book *The Coming of the French Revolution*, he knew he could not argue that the French working classes intended to form a communist party and establish a dictatorship of the proletariat. Such an anachronistic claim would not have been true to the experience of eighteenth-century French people, who had never heard of such things as the communist party or the dictatorship of the proletariat. Instead, Lefebvre gained a heightened awareness of class conflict from reading Marx, then used this awareness to ask new questions of his sources.[30]

Many students get interested in history because they want to understand the origins of something in the present. But it's essential to recognize that people who lived in the past almost certainly had different perspectives on their activities than modern researchers do. For example, although the origins of modern physics are commonly traced to Sir Isaac Newton (1643–1727), Newton's own thinking was heavily influenced by alchemy and theology—areas of study that may well seem bizarre from a modern scientific perspective. As Betty Jo Teeter Dobbs suggests in her book *The Janus Faces of Genius*, to understand the role that alchemy played in Newton's thought, the historian must "reconstruct . . . the lens through which Newton viewed himself".[31] It is perfectly legitimate to ask contemporary questions about former times, but historians must remain faithful to the perspectives of the people who lived in those times.

✑ REVIEW ❧

1. Think! What does your evidence tell you?
2. Think! What does your evidence not tell you?
3. Check facts carefully.
4. Compare evidence from a variety of sources.
5. Develop an argument based on all the evidence.
6. Be true to your characters' reality.

comes from your
own thinking

reflects the
evidence fairly

YOUR
THESIS

based on all
the evidence

INFERENCES

WHAT
DOES
IT ALL
MEAN?

THINK!

Continue to
search out and
read additional
materials,
check facts,
compare sources
and interpretations,
refine ideas

ᴄᴏ CHAPTER 4 ᴏᴠ

GET WRITING!

After days, weeks, or months of gathering and analyzing information, the time will finally come when you have to start writing. The transition from research to writing is often the most difficult stage of any project. Scholars facing a blank screen should heed the advice of Samuel Eliot Morison, one of the greatest historians of navigation. In an article entitled "History as a Literary Art: An Appeal to Young Historians," Morison urged students to resist the temptation to hunt down that one last source or to brew just one more pot of coffee. Morison insisted that his students "First and foremost, *get writing!*"[32]

Don't waste time wondering whether you have enough to say: if you have done your research thoroughly and really thought carefully about what you have learned, you will have plenty. And it doesn't matter if the writing is not perfect. You will find it much easier to correct mistakes in a draft than to come up with the material in the first place.

NARRATIVE AND ANALYSIS

So how do you start? First you need to find a suitable framework for your argument.

By now you have read a variety of sources, all of which have added to your knowledge and helped you to adjust and refine your ideas. Now your hypothesis has become a thesis: the main point of the argument that you will sustain throughout your essay. You also know which pieces of evidence you will be using to support that argument. But you may not know yet how you want to organize the essay: as one long narrative that touches on analytical topics, or as an analysis that uses short narratives to illustrate specific points. A good way to decide this crucial question is to create two short outlines, one for each approach.

DRAFT OUTLINE OF AN ANALYTICAL ESSAY

In the early stages of writing, it's usually helpful to create an outline that shows the broad lines of your argument, in order to test its feasibility.

Let's suppose that you have chosen to analyze the scientific response to Harrison's findings. This means that you are telling your story in order to examine an analytical problem. In that case your outline might look something like this:

I.   Introduction: non-scientific (social, cultural) influences on science
II. John Harrison
     A. His background
     B. His inventions
     C. The chronometer trials
III. Nevil Maskelyne
     A. His background
     B. His inventions
     C. His bias against Harrison
IV. Conclusion
     A. George III decides the case
     B. Significance of the case

Instead of telling a single narrative, this essay presents several short narratives and uses them to illustrate an analytical problem: the extent to which scientists may be biased by social or cultural factors.

COMPLETE ANALYTICAL OUTLINE

The draft outline above only provides a skeletal framework for an **analytical essay**. It may be useful as a beginning, but it doesn't do much to help you articulate your argument. To put some flesh on the bones, you need to add supporting points and details. The main point of the essay, the thesis, should be clearly stated in the introduction. The thesis statement sets up the whole paper, and everything that follows should be devoted to proving it. A complete outline of an analytical essay will show how you are moving from one analytical topic to another.

I.   Introduction: The scientific establishment of Harrison's day was reluctant to recognize his achievement. This illustrates how science is influenced by social and cultural factors. This topic is significant for two reasons:

    A.   Establishing longitude was a serious problem for navigators in the eighteenth century. We know this from the story of Anson's voyage of 1741.

    B.   A number of social scientists are now arguing that science reflects social and cultural influences, and we can use this case to test their position.

II.   John Harrison produced four marine chronometers, each of which met the criteria for winning the Longitude Prize.

    A.   Brief account of Harrison's modest background (son of a carpenter, little formal education) and the place of artisans in eighteenth-century English society. Brief description of Harrison's four chronometers (clocks), H-1, H-2, H-3, and H-4, and the mechanical innovations that would have qualified any one of them to win the prize.

    B.   The judges on the Board of Longitude refused to believe that he had solved the problem, even when the accuracy of his chronometers had been proven.

III.   Most of the Board members were astronomers: educated men who were not willing to accept a mechanical solution proposed by a simple clockmaker.

    A.   The place of astronomers in eighteenth-century English society and intellectual life, with specific reference to universities and government.

    B.   The astronomer Maskelyne's solution to the longitude problem, based on cumbersome mathematical tables that navigators could use to measure the distances from the moon to the planets and stars.

    C.   Maskelyne's behaviour during the trials of the clocks indicates sociocultural bias against Harrison.

IV. Conclusion: Harrison triumphs in spite of sociocultural obstacles.
- A. George III recognizes the superiority of Harrison's chronometers and intervenes on his behalf, but that intervention was largely a matter of luck.
- B. Social and cultural factors are deeply implicated in scientific and technological research.

This detailed outline is organized around analytical points, with evidence presented in short narrative accounts.

DRAFT OUTLINE OF A NARRATIVE ESSAY

It's also possible to organize an essay around a single chronological narrative, in this case an account of Harrison's life that includes important analytical points. Here is a simple draft outline of that **narrative essay**:

I.   Harrison's youth
- A. Education and training
- B. Awareness of longitude problem

II.   His solutions to the longitude problem
- A. Clock H-1
- B. Clock H-2
- C. Clock H-3
- D. Clock H-4

III.   Harrison at the end of his life
- A. Received award from Parliament rather than the Longitude Board
- B. Died.

COMPLETE NARRATIVE OUTLINE

A complete outline of a narrative essay on Harrison would include brief references to analytical issues:

I.   Harrison's youth: humble origins in Yorkshire and Lincolnshire, son of a carpenter. Touch on the place of such a family in English society (an analytical point).
   A. As a child, Harrison learned carpentry and taught himself rudimentary mathematics and physics—unusual for someone from his background.
   B. He built his first pendulum clock, incorporating new technical innovations.
   C. He was likely aware of the problems associated with calculating longitude, since this was a significant problem in eighteenth-century England.
II. Harrison's career as a clockmaker in London. Touch on the social status of artisans in London (another analytical point).
   A. Harrison built his first marine chronometer, H-1, and during the trials had his first encounters with naval officers and astronomers. Comment on the social and cultural differences between the latter and Harrison.
   B. Harrison built H-2 and H-3, solving numerous technical problems. But relations with the astronomers, especially Maskelyne, deteriorated. Provide some social and educational background on Maskelyne.
   C. Harrison built H-4, a totally new design for a marine chronometer that deserved to win the Longitude Prize. Serious clashes with Maskelyne illustrate the influence of the relations between science and culture (an analytical point).
III. The end of Harrison's life
   A. Harrison was dissatisfied by his treatment at the hands of the Longitude Board.
   B. George III intervened on his behalf and Parliament agreed to a financial reward, but the official Longitude Prize was never awarded. Harrison died. End with a reflection on what his story suggests about the influence on science of social and cultural factors.

This detailed outline shows how a straightforward chronological narrative can incorporate important analytical content.

◌◌ REVIEW ◌◌

1. Create an outline for either an analytical or a narrative paper.
2. If in doubt, create a second outline, from a different angle. Then see which one works best.
3. Structure your paper to suit your purpose and evidence.

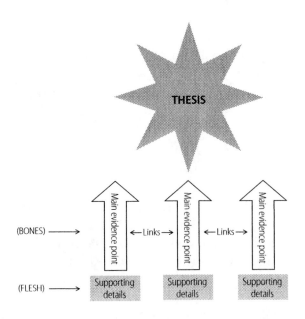

ᴄ CHAPTER 5 ᴏ

REPORTING FAITHFULLY

In the first century BCE, the Roman statesman Cicero laid down two laws for the historian:

> The first . . . is that he shall never dare utter an untruth. The second is that he shall suppress nothing that is true.[33]

These laws remain in force. But good historians also ask questions, and one question comes immediately to mind: how do historians know what is true in any given case? There is no easy answer. Inevitably, some evidence disappears, different sources often contradict one another, and the "truth" can quite legitimately depend on the point of view of the reporter. For example, the missionaries who introduced Christianity to Aboriginal societies may have sincerely believed that they were giving them an incomparable gift. Those societies, however, may have experienced that "gift" as something quite different.

Thus the best we can do is to ensure that we follow a few basic rules in our own work to arrive at an answer that fully reflects the available evidence. Like the law, the rules for faithful representation of the past are subject to variation and interpretation over time, and historical writers do not take a Hippocratic oath to uphold any particular body of rules. Nevertheless, there is a broad general consensus about what is right and what is wrong.

REPORT SOURCES CAREFULLY

All scholars build on the work of others. Therefore it is essential to be able to trust that other historians have been faithful to their sources. Above all, it is important to report accurately on the people and events of the past. Sloppy note-taking can lead you to misrepresent history, and readers may accuse you of dishonesty even if the misrepresentation is inadvertent. One way to avoid misunderstanding is to follow these rules:

1. *Make sure that every note you take includes a citation.* Every time you jot down a note, write the bibliographic reference next to it. Include as much of the following information as is applicable: full name of author, complete title (including subtitle), series title, edition and volume number, place of publication, publisher, year of publication, and page number. Whatever medium you use—paper, index cards, or computer—every piece of information should be accompanied by the relevant source reference. Even if you're pressed for time, don't cut corners in your notes: instead, figure out a way to be more efficient. For instance, you could set up a system of abbreviations, or collect all notes from each source together under one bibliographical entry, with a page number for each item, or use colour coding.

2. *Distinguish clearly between your own words and those of someone else.* Always put direct quotations in quotation marks. When you paraphrase (reword) or summarize someone else's material, make sure that you will recognize your own words.

3. *Copy and paste with care.* Before the age of the personal computer, writing and revising a paper was in some ways a more demanding task than it is today. Even so, word processing technology does present some new organizational challenges. Be especially careful, when copying text from the Internet, that you don't accidentally paste it into your draft paper rather than your notes: if you do, you'll run the risk of confusing someone else's words with your own. Always keep your notes in a separate file—and be sure to record the source of any research material that you find online.

    Writing technology has changed, but the prohibition on **plagiarism** has not.[34] Since your professor may ask to see your notes and drafts, it's a good idea to print out hard copy of in-progress work as you go along (or at least to save each successive draft under a different file name). Be sure to keep all your notes and drafts until the paper has been graded and returned to you.

TREAT OTHERS' IDEAS WITH CARE AND RESPECT

Researching and writing papers means engaging with the ideas of fellow scholars. As a student you will spend much, if not all, of your time interpreting subjects that many others have interpreted before you. Even if you are the first person to write a history of something, in order to show its full significance, you will have to place your own ideas in the context of a broader historical literature.

Writing is hard work. Therefore it is important to acknowledge the work of others in a respectful way. Historians have conventions for quoting, summarizing, and paraphrasing the works of other scholars. If you follow these conventions faithfully, you won't have to go back and check your sources again while you are writing.

PARAPHRASES AND SUMMARIES

Technically speaking, a **paraphrase** uses roughly the same number of words as the original passage, whereas a **summary** uses fewer. Paraphrase is useful when you want to discuss an idea from someone else's work but think that you can say the same thing more clearly. It can be particularly helpful when you need to translate an archaic or complex quotation. In *The Reluctant Land*, Cole Harris uses both quotation and paraphrase to introduce a concept from the German philosopher Jürgen Habermas:

> In premodern societies, he [Habermas] maintains, people lived "within the horizons of their lifeworld" and could not reach beyond its preinterpreted understandings. In other words, they could interpret and communicate the world only within their own terms of reference.[35]

Summaries are more common than paraphrases in historical writing. They are particularly useful in works of synthesis, where the author engages with other authors and needs to present their ideas in concise form. In a recent collection of articles entitled *The Conquest of Acadia*,

1710, Maurice Basque summarizes the work of John Bartlet Brebner (1895–1957), the historian who coined the term "North Atlantic Triangle":

> Generations of historians have been influenced by John Bartlet Brebner's reading of Acadians' reaction to military and political events, specifically that Acadian society was not politically minded.

Basque then summarizes some of Brebner's evidence and discusses his influence on the work of other historians. He also provides citations for further exploration.[36] Summaries can also be useful when the original material is problematic in some way (for instance, if the language is archaic or overly technical). Both summaries and paraphrases indicate to the reader that you have grasped someone else's idea so well that you are able to convey it in your own words. In either case, be sure to include all the relevant points made in the original passage.

DIRECT QUOTATIONS

Historians usually demonstrate their familiarity with sources by summarizing and paraphrasing, but sometimes they find that a direct quotation is the best way to make a point. Use a direct quotation when correct interpretation depends on the exact wording of the source, or when the original is so effective—so vivid or forceful—that a paraphrase or summary could not do it justice. Otherwise, try to limit your use of quotations. After all, it's your own ideas that the reader wants to find out about.

There are two ways of incorporating quotations. Typically, a short quotation will be run into in the main text as part of a sentence that identifies the source. Thus if you were writing about the history of gay rights in Canada, you might quote Pierre Trudeau:

> In 1967, Trudeau remarked that "there's no place for the state in the bedrooms of the nation."

Notice that in this example, the quotation is not separated from the body of the sentence by either a comma or a colon. Punctuation should be used only when the grammatical structure of the sentence requires it:

> As Trudeau remarked in 1967, "there's no place for the state in the bedrooms of the nation."

The second approach is normally reserved for passages of more than three lines. A **block quotation** is set off from the main text in a separate block indented 10 spaces from the left margin, with a line space above and below. The sentence before the quotation should introduce it, and the sentence after it should link the quotation to the text that follows. For example, in *Lethal Legacy: Current Native Controversies in Canada*, J.R. Miller quotes from the section of the Royal Proclamation of 1763 that was designed to prevent unscrupulous buyers from cheating Aboriginal peoples out of their lands:

> Too often Thirteen Colonies purchasers could brandish their "deed" and insist that the state help to enforce their spurious title against indigenous resistance. The Royal Proclamation aimed to prevent such outrages by decreeing that private citizens could not obtain Native land.
>
> > And whereas Great Frauds and Abuses have been committed in purchasing Land of the Indians, to the great Prejudice of our Interests, and to the great Dissatisfaction of the said Indians; In order, therefore, to prevent such Irregularities for the future, and to the End that the Indians may be convinced of our Justice and determined Resolution to remove all reasonable Cause of Discontent, We do, with the Advice of our Privy Council strictly enjoin and require, that no private Person do presume to make any Purchase from the said Indians of any Lands reserved to the said Indians. . . .
>
> Only the Crown could legally get land from Aboriginal people. And, even then, the Crown's representative had to do so in a public way. Said the Proclamation, if "any of the said Indians should be inclined to dispose of the said Lands, the same shall be Purchased only for Us in our Name, at some public Meeting or Assembly of the said Indians, to be held for the Purpose by the Governor or Commander in Chief of our Colony."[37]

In this case, the paragraphs that precede and follow the quotation seamlessly integrate it into Miller's text.

BE FAIR TO YOUR SOURCES

Historians often need to abridge the passages they quote in order to make them fit into their own material. To indicate omissions they use ellipsis points, which look like three periods (. . .). One basic rule governs the use of **ellipses**: any abridged quotation must be faithful to the original, full quotation.

This is not as easy as it sounds. Suppose you are writing a five-page essay on the 1837 rebellion in Upper Canada and have decided to focus on the reformers' complaints concerning Britain's treatment of the colony. In a newspaper article most likely written by William Lyon Mackenzie they enumerated a long list of grievances, which included the following:

- The King of England has forbidden his governors to pass laws of immediate and pressing importance, unless suspended in their operation till his assent should be obtained; and when so suspended, he has utterly neglected to attend to them. He has interfered with the freedom of elections, and appointed elections to be held at places dangerous, unconvenient and unsafe for the people to assemble at, for the purpose of fatiguing them into his measures, through the agency of pretended representatives; and has through his legislative council, prevented provision from being made for quiet and peaceable elections, as in the case of the late returns at Beverley.
- He has dissolved the late House of Assembly for opposing with manly firmness Sir Francis Head's invasion of the right of the people to a wholesome control over the revenue, and for insisting that the persons conducting the government should be responsible for their official conduct to the country through its representatives.
- He has endeavoured to prevent the peopling of this province and its advancement in wealth; for that purpose obstructing the

laws for the naturalization of foreigners, refusing to pass others to encourage their migration hither, and raising the conditions of new appropriations of the public lands, large tracts of which he has bestowed upon unworthy persons his favourites, while deserving settlers from Germany and other countries have been used cruelly.

• He has rendered the administration of Justice liable to suspicion and distrust, by obstructing laws for establishing a fair trial by Jury, by refusing to exclude the chief criminal judge from interfering in political business, and by selecting as the judiciary violent and notorious partisans of his arbitrary power.[38]

Mackenzie's language is so rich that you would like to quote the entire document, but that would take up too much of your limited space. Therefore you decide to abridge his text, using ellipses to indicate omissions:

> Enumerating their complaints in a newspaper article (most likely written by Mackenzie), the reformers charged that "The King of England has forbidden his governors to pass laws of immediate and pressing importance, unless suspended in their operation till his assent should be obtained. . . . He has interfered with the freedom of elections. . . . He has dissolved the late House of Assembly. . . . He has endeavoured to prevent the peopling of this province and its advancement in wealth. . . . He has rendered the administration of Justice liable to suspicion and distrust. . . ."

But notice that your sentence does not flow well into the quotation: there is a jarring difference between your verb tense and Mackenzie's. You could eliminate the problem by removing the word "has," except that then you'd be stuck with the incorrect form of the verb "to forbid." In addition, writing "King William" and then having the quotation repeat "he" as the subject sounds awkward and unnatural. You could solve these problems by inserting some bracketed words so that your sentence flows naturally into the quotation from Mackenzie. The brackets tell readers that these are not Mackenzie's exact words, but that they still convey Mackenzie's exact meaning

In a newspaper article that was most likely written by Mackenzie the reformers listed a number of complaints about Britain's treatment of Upper Canada. They charged that that "the King . . . [had] forbidden his governors to pass laws of immediate and pressing importance, unless suspended in their operation till his assent should be obtained . . . interfered with the freedom of elections . . . dissolved the late House of Assembly . . . endeavoured to prevent the peopling of . . . [the] province and its advancement in wealth . . . [and] rendered the administration of justice liable to suspicion and distrust. . . ."

This quotation is faithful to Mackenzie's exact meaning, even though it abridges his text with ellipses and brackets. Not every abridgement is so faithful, however. It would have been unfaithful to use ellipses in the following manner: "The King of England has forbidden his governors to pass laws of immediate and pressing importance . . . for the purpose of fatiguing [the people] into his measures." This version would be unfair to Mackenzie, because the first portion of the original quotation actually introduced an entirely different set of ideas: "unless suspended in their operation till his assent should be obtained; and when so suspended, he has utterly neglected to attend to them."

In the same way, it would have been unfaithful to write "The King of England has forbidden his governors to pass necessary laws . . ." because you would be altering the sense of the original text: "He has forbidden his governors to pass laws of immediate and pressing importance . . ." If you need to be so concise, summarizing Mackenzie in your own words would be preferable to inserting different words directly into his original writing.

USING QUOTATION MARKS

Quotation marks seem to cause more confusion than any other form of punctuation (with the possible exception of apostrophes). When you run a quotation into your text, place the words inside double quotation marks:

Borden called Canada "a nation that is not a nation."

For a quotation within a quotation, use single quotation marks:

> In her account of the post-First World War Paris Peace Conference, *Paris 1919: Six Months That Changed the World*, Margaret MacMillan writes that Canadian Prime Minister Borden saw "Canada as 'a nation that is not a nation,' a situation he hoped 'to alter.'"[39]

The placement of other punctuation in relation to the quotation marks varies. Periods and commas should be placed *inside* the quotation marks. However, question marks and exclamation points should be placed *outside* unless they were part of the original quotation. Colons and semicolons also go outside the quotation marks.

DON'T PLAGIARIZE

Unfaithful quotation is a serious problem, but the harshest condemnation is reserved for plagiarists. In the ancient Mediterranean world, *plagiarii* were pirates whose crimes included the kidnapping of young children.[40] When plagiarists claim someone else's ideas as their own, they steal someone else's brainchild. Historians do not tolerate this behaviour. In their efforts to combat plagiarism, some universities require that students submit their papers to text-matching software, and most enforce severe disciplinary policies. At the very least, the plagiarist will fail the assignment in question, but the penalties can include expulsion from the university and a record of the offence on the student's permanent record.

Plagiarism is infrequent among professional scholars, who share a commitment to honesty across all the disciplines. Even so, it does occur from time to time.

1. *Direct plagiarism.* Direct plagiarism occurs when one writer takes another writer's exact words and passes them off as his or her own. Direct plagiarism is usually easy for an informed reader to spot.

2. **Indirect plagiarism.** Indirect plagiarism is more difficult to recognize. It occurs when writers paraphrase someone else's work too closely. In such cases the plagiarist inserts an occasional new word or phrase to make the writing slightly different, but retains the original structure of the sentence or paragraph. For example, here is an original passage taken from Colin M. Coates' article "Commemorating the Woman Warrior of New France, Madeleine de Verchères, 1696–1930." Discussing a monument to de Verchères, Coates writes:

> Gazing upon the statue . . . , no one would mistake her for a man: the swirling dress, the feminine facial features, the long braids dangling down her back, the pubescent breasts, all precluded misinterpretation. Only her (men's) hat and massive gun hinted otherwise.[41]

The following overly close paraphrase would amount to indirect plagiarism:

> Looking at the memorial, no observer could take her for a male. Her womanly clothes and appearance would prevent any mistake. Nothing but her hat and gun suggested masculinity.

This would be indirect plagiarism even if it were accompanied by a citation acknowledging Coates's work, because the writer does not clearly indicate how much has been borrowed from it.

Here is an example of an acceptable paraphrase:

> Colin Coates remarks that this is clearly a statue of a woman, arguing that the clothes and personal appearance, in fact everything except the "hat and massive gun," make it impossible to think otherwise.

With the appropriate citation, the explicit reference to Coates makes the source of the sentence perfectly clear.

3. **Inadvertent plagiarism.** What if you accidentally neglect to put quotation marks around a passage from someone else's writing? What if you forget to provide a citation when you summarize someone else's writing? Think for a minute about your readers. All they see are the words in front of them. They don't see you

frantically trying to finish your essay at two in the morning. By the time you apologize for the oversight, it will be too late. When readers detect a mistake, they will instinctively form the worst possible impression of you.

In 2002, two prominent historians, Stephen Ambrose and Doris Kearns Goodwin, were accused of plagiarism. Both defended themselves by admitting to sloppy research practices. This is a believable defence, but it is also deeply embarrassing, and the careers of both authors were damaged. The "sloppiness" defence highlights the relationship between plagiarism and lack of discipline.

Try to avoid situations that may be conducive to plagiarism. Don't wait until the last minute to research and write historical essays. Make sure that you have plenty of time to document your sources correctly and double-check them to make sure, even when you are certain that everything is in order. You may be surprised at how often you will find little mistakes.

It's your responsibility to use your sources honestly and fairly, and "I didn't mean to" is no excuse. To make matters worse, it will be much easier for readers to prove your guilt than for you to prove your innocence.

4. *Academic dishonesty.* It goes without saying that you should never submit anything with your name on it that was written by somebody else. This includes any paper bought from an essay writing service, downloaded (even in part) from the Internet, or found in a fraternity file. If you pass off someone else's work as your own, you are a plagiarist. According to most university regulations, anyone who supplies you with such a paper is a plagiarist as well.

    There are other acts of academic dishonesty that closely resemble plagiarism. Occasionally it may be possible to submit the same paper in two courses, but only if you have obtained permission in advance from both instructors: otherwise you will be passing off as original work something that is not. In addition, an instructor's permission is usually required if you want to submit a paper written in collaboration with another student. If you are allowed to work with another student, you must never try pass off the other student's writing as your own.

DON'T GIVE UNNECESSARY CITATIONS

After reading the preceding section, are you now so frightened that you feel you have to include a source citation in every sentence you write? If so, remember that the purpose of the essay is to set out your ideas. The main argument is expected to be yours and should need no notes.

Don't go overboard with citations. Provide them only when you cite statistics or obscure facts, when you quote directly, paraphrase, or summarize someone else's work, or when you are consciously borrowing the structure of someone else's approach to a topic. There is no need to provide a citation for a fact that is common knowledge: for example, that the Allies landed at Normandy on 6 June 1944, or that the CPR played a crucial part in the settlement of western Canada.

There is also no need to provide a citation for more specialized knowledge that is familiar to anyone working "within the field." For example, most people probably do not know the dates and dynasties of the Roman emperors, but this is common knowledge to historians of the Roman world, and not particularly open to interpretation or disagreement. Of course, if you are unsure whether something is common knowledge, there's no harm in playing it safe and providing a citation.[42]

CHOOSE A CITATION SYSTEM THAT SUITS YOUR READERS

There are only two rules that apply to all source citations: the format you choose must make it easy for readers to check your sources, and you must use it consistently. Otherwise the rules vary widely, partly because many publishers have their own "house styles" and partly because individual institutions, departments, and even instructors often have their own preferred style guides. If your professor has not specified a **citation system**, be sure to ask what is expected.

Students are sometimes confused to find that that their history instructor will not accept the citation system they have been taught in other courses. For example, the standard approach in sociology is to place the author's name, date of publication, and page number in parentheses after a quotation, summary, or paraphrase. Although this system can work well in some cases, most historians use sequential footnotes or endnotes, following the guidelines laid out in Kate L. Turabian, *A Manual for Writers of Term Papers, Theses, and Dissertations*, 7th ed. (Chicago: University of Chicago Press, 2007). "Turabian," as it is usually called, is a concise version of the rules set out in the *Chicago Manual of Style*, which is widely considered the authoritative guide for preparing manuscripts.[43] Both books can be found in any academic library.

The reason historians tend to prefer the notes and bibliography system is that their source references are often too long and complex to fit neatly into a parenthetical citation. Not only are sources such as letters and diaries difficult to cite concisely, but historians frequently refer to more than one source at a time. To include so much information in the text would be distracting and annoying for readers. Thus most history instructors prefer that students use either footnotes or endnotes, both of which are easy to create using a word-processing program. If the source you are working with does not fit any of the models outlined here, refer to either Turabian or the *Chicago Manual*.

FOOTNOTES AND ENDNOTES

The only difference between footnotes and **endnotes** is their placement: footnotes go at the bottom of the page and endnotes at the end of the paper. Otherwise they are identical. Their purpose is to tell readers exactly where you found your material. They should include all the information necessary for readers to look up your sources themselves and evaluate your use of them.

Every time you quote, paraphrase, summarize, or otherwise refer to someone else's material or ideas, create a note with a **superscript number** in the text. Start with number 1 at the beginning of the paper and keep going: don't start again with number 1 at the top of each page (or the beginning of each new section), and don't use the same number every time you refer to the same source.

When you read, you will find that note references are usually placed at the end of the sentence: "J.R. Miller argues that the First Nations peoples in Canada consistently sought to determine their own paths."[4] The number belongs at the end of the sentence, rather than following Miller's name, because the entire sentence concerns his book *Skyscrapers Hide the Heavens*, 3rd ed. (Toronto: University of Toronto Press, 2000). The only time it might be appropriate to place the note in the middle of a sentence would be if the latter part of the sentence referred to a second author and it was necessary to distinguish the two.

1. ***Formatting footnotes and endnotes.*** Most word-processing programs today now handle references automatically: all you have to do is select the appropriate format (footnote or endnote; number style) and specify where each note should be inserted. Notes should be single-spaced in the same font size as the main text, and each note is generally formatted as a single sentence, punctuated with commas and colons. The first line of the note begins with an indentation from the left margin. After the note number, insert a period and a space.

2. ***Citing a book.*** Endnotes and footnotes to books should be written like this:

   4. John Mack Farragher, *A Great and Noble Scheme: The Tragic Story of the Expulsion of the Acadians from Their American Homeland* (New York: Norton, 2005), 35–39.

   The author's first name comes first, information about the publisher is placed in parentheses, and a comma precedes the page numbers. There is usually no need for a "p." or "pp." in front of the page numbers, unless there is some risk of confusion with other numbers in the citation.

3. ***Citing different kinds of books.*** Not all books have such simple publication information. In fact, the possible permutations are endless. The following examples cover some of the standard book types: a multi-author book, a multi-volume book, an edited volume, and a revised edition.

11. Sally Ross and Alphonse Deveau, *The Acadians of Nova Scotia Past and Present* (Halifax: Nimbus, 1992), 73.

12. J. Murray Beck, *Joseph Howe*, 2 vols. (Kingston and Montreal: McGill-Queen's University Press, 1982), 2: 133.

13. *The Conquest of Acadia, 1710*, ed. John G. Reid, Maurice Basque, et al. (Toronto: University of Toronto Press, 2004), 48–63.

14. Alan D. McMillan, *Native Peoples and Culture of Canada: An Anthropological Overview*, 2nd ed. (Vancouver and Toronto: Douglas & McIntyre, 1995), 113.

4. *Citing scholarly articles.* Scholarly articles by historians are usually published in either scholarly journals or edited collections. Note that article titles are placed in quotation marks. The form for an edited collection resembles a book citation:

> 37.   M.A. Kalbach and Warren E. Kalbach, "Demographic Overview of Ethnic Origin Groups in Canada," in *Race and Ethnic Relations in Canada*, 2nd ed., ed. Peter S. Li (Don Mills, ON: Oxford University Press, 1999), 251.

Journal articles are cited somewhat differently. The author and title are given first, followed by the title of the journal, its volume and number, the date in parentheses, and a colon followed by the page number. Here is a simple citation, followed by one that is more complex.

> 38. Janice Potter, "Patriarchy and Paternalism: the Case of the Eastern Ontario Loyalist Women," *Ontario History* 81, 1 (March 1989): 17.
>
> 39. Janet Floyd, "'I Am a Gleaner': Catharine Parr Traill and *Forest Gleanings*," *British Journal of Canadian Studies* 17, 1 (2004): 97.

Ordinarily, an article title is simply placed in quotation marks, followed by the italicized (or underlined) journal title and the publication information. In the example above, however, the first part of the title is a quotation itself, placed in single quotation marks within the double quotation marks. If the quotation were of a book title rather than simply a phrase, the book title would be underlined or italicized.

5. *Citing works of journalism.* Citations of articles in newspapers and magazines should provide the name of the author, article title, name of the magazine or newspaper, date, section (for a newspaper), and page number. For example,

> 40. Bob Levin and Rae Corelli, "The Tracks of History," *Maclean's*, 6 July 1992, 18.

6. *Citing unpublished secondary works.* Sometimes, in the course of your research, you may come across an unpublished secondary work, such as a thesis or dissertation that could be a useful source. If you do, ask your librarian if you need the author's permission to read or cite it. Theses and dissertations are cited as follows:

> 8. Nanci Delayen, "The Fabian Society and Eugenics, 1885–1914" (MA thesis, University of Saskatchewan, 1998), 57.

Historians often circulate unpublished papers or manuscripts among their colleagues. Professional courtesy dictates that these may be used and cited only with the author's permission:

> 33. William K. Storey, "Science and the Making of a British Ideology of Development in Post-Emancipation Barbados" (unpublished manuscript in the author's possession), 14.

7. *Citing interviews, lectures, and oral presentations.* These kinds of citations should give the name of the source and the place and date on which he or she gave you the information. Courtesy dictates that private conversations should not be cited unless you have the permission of the person you interviewed. See the section on "oral history projects" in Chapter 11 (p. 127) for more information on oral history.

> 76. Ernest Hemingway, interview with the author, Key West, Florida, 6 September 1932.

8. *Citing archival sources.* Every archive is organized differently, so the main rule for archival citations is to provide all the information necessary for a reader to trace your source. Fortunately,

some institutions provide researchers with guidelines for citing material from their collections. Among them is Britain's National Archives, which in 2003 took over what was formerly known as the Public Records Office (PRO). The following citation directs readers to the PRO section of the National Archives Colonial Office (CO) files, item number 167/661:

> 61. Lees to Knutsford, with minutes by Wingfield, 9 Jan. 1891, National Archives: PRO CO 167/661.

If you are conducting research in an archive, be sure to ask if there is a correct way to cite their sources. Also be sure to spell out any abbreviations the first time you use them, so that your readers will know what they mean.

9.   *Citing Internet sources.* References to web sources follow the same principles as any other citation: they should give readers all the information they need to find those sources themselves. Thus Internet citations should give the full Universal Resource Locator (URL) address of the page where the material was found, not just the relevant home page.

At the same time it is important to acknowledge that, whereas print sources are more or less permanent and can almost always be located in a major research library, Internet sources can change or disappear at any time. Therefore it is essential to record the date when you accessed the material, along with the date of publication if it is available. It's also advisable to keep a printout of every web page you cite from the day when you used it: that way, if a reader challenges your use of the material, you will have the evidence even if the page has changed or disappeared.

Of course, your citation should also include the author, title, and whatever additional information is available. Thus to cite an article from an online version of a print journal, you would begin in exactly the same way you would for a conventional print article, listing the author, title, journal, issue number, and date. Then list the date of access, followed by a comma, and finally the URL.

Now suppose you wanted to cite some archival material—specifically, an article that appeared in the (Victoria) *British Colonist* in 1869—that you found on the website called *Who Killed William Robinson?* Created by Ruth Sandwell and John Lutz, this site is now part of the "Great Unsolved Mysteries in Canadian History Project." For each mystery, the site reproduces many primary and secondary sources, including newspaper articles, photographs, legal documents, correspondence, diaries, artists' reconstructions, paintings, and historians' commentaries. Use the following method to cite an archival newspaper article from the *Robinson* site:

> 42. "Threats," *British Colonist*, 3 June 1869. *Who Killed William Robinson?* (website), Ruth Sandwell and John Lutz, accessed 17 August 2010, http://www.canadianmysteries.ca/sites/robinson/home/indexen.html.

If you know the newspaper page and column number, include it after the publication date. Note that in some cases a website will provide only one main address, as shown on its home pages. Some sites show individual addresses for each section or document, so be sure to check carefully for these and to include them where appropriate.

10. ***How to repeat a citation.*** In the past, most writers used Latin abbreviations such as *ibid.* ("the same"), *loc. cit.* ("in the place cited"), and *op. cit.* ("in the work cited") to indicate repeated references to the same source. Today, some writers still use *ibid.* when two consecutive notes cite exactly the same source, right down to the page number, but most prefer a simpler system. The first time you cite a source, give the full citation; then for subsequent references give only the author's last name, a short version of the title, and the page number(s). Here are some examples:

> 11. J.I. Little, *Borderland Religion: The Emergence of an English-Canadian Identity, 1792–1852* (Toronto: University of Toronto Press, 2004), 45.
> 12. Little, *Borderland*, 73.

13. David R. Cameron and Graham White, *Getting Into Saigon: The Conservative Transition in Ontario* (Vancouver: University of British Columbia Press, 2000), 124.

14. Cameron and White, *Getting Into Saigon*, 91.

15. Little, *Borderland*, 14.

16. Ibid.

17. Cameron and White, *Getting Into Saigon*, 63–65.

If you decide to use *ibid.*, be extra careful at the revision stage: it's easy to separate consecutive entries when you are moving material around.

11. ***Citing a quotation of a quotation.*** Historians prefer to quote from original sources. If you see a primary source quotation in a secondary work and you want to quote it as well, you are expected to check the primary source and assess the accuracy of the quotation yourself.

Sometimes, though, you may not have access to the original source. Suppose you have read about the execution of Louis XVI in Simon Schama's book *Citizens: A Chronicle of the French Revolution*. Schama quotes from a memoir by Louis-Sébastien Mercier:

> His blood flowed and cries of joy from eighty thousand armed men struck my ears. . . . I saw the schoolboys of the Quatre-Nations throw their hats in the air; his blood flowed and some dipped their fingers in it, or a pen or a piece of paper; one tasted it and said *Il est bougrement salé . . .*

Now you want to use this colourful passage in your own work, but have not been able to track down a copy of the original work. You can still use the quotation if you attribute it as follows:

27. Louis-Sébastien Mercier, as cited in Simon Schama, *Citizens: A Chronicle of the French Revolution* (New York: Knopf, 1989), 670.

Note that the author is correctly listed as Mercier, even though you read the passage in a book by Schama.

12. ***Discursive notes.*** In the course of your reading, you may notice that some authors use endnotes or footnotes not only to cite

their sources but to address points of interpretation, or even to digress from their subjects. These discursive notes can be useful to the author, but readers often find them annoying. If something is important enough to say, why not say it in the main body of the text? Think carefully before introducing a discursive note: don't use it as a way to sneak additional material into the paper without exceeding your page limit.

13. ***Know the difference between notes and bibliographies.*** Unless your paper is very short, it will usually require a bibliography: an alphabetical list of all the sources you consulted in preparing it. Bibliography entries are in some ways similar in form to notes. However, the main elements of each entry are separated with periods rather than commas and parentheses, and the author's name is reversed, last name first (if there is more than one author, the others' names are not reversed). For an article, inclusive page numbers should follow the issue number. Bibliographies also usually have a hanging indent, meaning that the first line of an entry is five spaces to the left of the following lines:

> Binnema, Theodore. *Common and Contested Ground: A Human and Environmental History of the Northwestern Plains.* Norman: University of Oklahoma Press, 2001.
>
> Hogue, Michael. "Disputing the Medicine Line: The Plains Cree and the Canadian-American Border, 1876–85." In *One West, Two Myths*, edited by Carol Higham and Robert Thacker, 85–108. Calgary: University of Calgary Press, 2004.
>
> Ray, Arthur J., Jim Miller, and Frank Tough. *Bounty and Benevolence: a Documentary History of Saskatchewan Treaties.* Kingston and Montreal: McGill-Queen's University Press, 2000.
>
> Vogt, David and David Alexander Gamble. 'You Don't Suppose the Dominion Government Wants to Cheat the Indians?' The Grand Trunk Pacific Railway and the Fort George Reserve." *BC Studies* 166 (Summer 2010): 55–72.

For other questions about notes and bibliographies, see either Turabian or the *Chicago Manual*, both of which offer much more comprehensive

To show some "real life" referencing, here is an excerpt from a recent undergraduate paper on the history of the Britannia Beach mines in British Columbia, by Justin Elsworth:

> While the natives used "copper for decorations [such as] ear spools, beads, and . . . sheets of copper used in potlatches,"[1] some native legends say Britannia was never fished or hunted at because it was cursed.[2] Such a curse holds true for one of the first discoverers of Britannia, a fur trapper named Oliver Furry, who had been drawn to the area by the BC Gold Rush. Furry made claims in the Jane Basin area with a man named Joseph Boscowitz in 1898, but returned in 1901 to find that 7/10ths interest in the Boscowitz holdings had been sold for $35,000 to Howard Walters of Montana.[3] Engaged in legal disputes over Britannia, Furry became increasingly violent because of stress over the claim of ownership and was ultimately institutionalized in New Westminster.[4] In a cruel twist of fate, the courts ruled that Furry had "held a fifty percent interest"[5] in 1906, but unfortunately Furry had died the previous year in the asylum. Furry, like so many others during the BC Gold Rush era, would never prosper from his finds.

Here are the footnote or endnote references for this excerpt:

1. Florida Ann Town, *The Lively Ghost of Howe Sound* (Port Coquitlam, BC: Bookus Press, 2000), 4.
2. *Britannia: A Company Town*, VHS, directed by David Vaisbord (Montreal: National Film Board of Canada, 2000).
3. Town, *Lively Ghost*, 23.
4. Doreen Armitage, *Around the Howe Sound: A History of Howe Sound-Whistler* (Madeira Park, BC: Harbour Publishing, 1997), 102.
5. Bruce Ramsey, *Britannia: The Story of a Mine*, 2nd. ed. (Victoria: Britannia Beach Historical Society, 2004), 26.

Here are the bibliography entries for the same sources:

Armitage, Doreen. *Around the Howe Sound: A History of Howe Sound-Whistler*. Madeira Park, BC: Harbour Publishing, 1997.
Britannia: A Company Town. Directed by David Vaisbord. Montreal: National Film Board of Canada, 2000. Videocassette.
Ramsey, Bruce. *Britannia: The Story of a Mine*. Victoria: Britannia Beach Historical Society, 2004.
Town, Florida Ann. *The Lively Ghost of Howe Sound*. Port Coquitlam, BC: Bookus Press, 2000.

listings. They also cover the in-text author–date citation systems that are more commonly used in literature and the social sciences, notably the Modern Language Association (MLA) style and the American Psychological Association (APA) style. Note that the fifth edition of the MLA *Handbook* includes an appendix on endnotes and footnotes.

✸ REVIEW ✸

1. Record and report your sources with care.
2. When you paraphrase or summarize someone else's argument, make it clear.
3. Use the appropriate citation system.
4. Don't forget the bibliography.

CHAPTER 6

BUILD AN ARGUMENT

A historical essay needs to do more than state a thesis and present evidence to support it. A good historical essay will lead its readers through its argument so persuasively that they will convinced of the truth of your conclusion. An argument is not a dispute or disagreement: it is an idea that is developed over the course of an essay. An argument must capture and hold the reader's attention.

START TO WRITE A FIRST DRAFT

The complete outlines in Chapter 4 are the frameworks for two sustained arguments. A good outline will show how each section of the essay is related to the main argument. As you are thinking about the overall outline of your essay, check your sources for evidence supporting your thesis, and compose paragraphs around those points. You don't have to start with the introduction; in fact, you may well write it last. As you grapple with your sources, you will discover new things about them, things that may make your first version of the introduction obsolete by the time you finish the body of the text.

While you are writing the first draft, adding analysis and information, stand back occasionally and think about how your argument is evolving. Is it developing in a reasonable way? If not—if you find that you have modified your line of argument in some way—don't worry. Just go back to the beginning, adjust your thesis statement if necessary, and then check the entire argument for consistency.

GRAB YOUR READER'S ATTENTION, BUT DO IT GENTLY

Every reader asks, "Why should I read this?" "Why should I care?" Writers must give their readers reasons to care. Many historians use the beginning of an essay or book to connect their scholarly interests to broader academic and political debates. For example, in a 1997 article called "Taming Aboriginal Sexuality: Gender, Power and Race in British Columbia, 1850–1900," Jean Barman begins with a courtroom scene and frames it in a way that is bound to grab the reader's attention:

> In July 1996 I listened in a Vancouver court room as Catholic Bishop Hubert O'Conner defended himself against charges of having raped or indecently assaulted four young Aboriginal women three decades earlier. His assertion of ignorance when asked what one of the complainants had been wearing on the grounds that "as you know, I'm a celibate man" encapsulated his certainty that he had done nothing wrong. He admitted to sexual relations with two of the women, but the inference was clear: they had made him do it. They had dragged him down and led him astray. The temptation exercised by their sexuality was too great for any mere man, even a priest and residential school principal, to resist.
>
> I returned home from that day, and subsequent days in the court room, deeply troubled. I might have been reading any of hundreds of similar accounts written over the past century and more about Aboriginal women in British Columbia. This essay represents my first attempt to come to terms with Bishop O'Conner and his predecessors. . . . My interest is not in Bishop O'Conner's guilt or innocence in a court of law, but, rather, in tracing the lineage of his attitudes in the history of British Columbia.[44]

Notice Barman's tone. She addresses topics of universal interest like sex and racism, and specific incidents that could cause revulsion, but she does so calmly and methodically. You don't need to drop a bomb to get your reader's attention, and you don't need to be emotional or sensationalist. Be relevant, but be gentle. Readers prefer writing that they find balanced, trustworthy, and authoritative. If you suspect that they may disagree with you, it's your job to bring them around. Put them in the right frame of mind to listen to your argument.

STATE YOUR INTELLECTUAL INTERESTS EARLY

In the example above, Barman first catches the reader's attention by frankly stating the disturbing facts of the case. She then quickly shifts the focus and begins to outline her intellectual interest in it. Your readers will also expect you to give them a sense of your intellectual interests. What are the broader historical problems that your essay addresses? Why have you chosen your specific topic to explore those interests? What argument will you be developing over the course of your essay? If you don't address these questions at the beginning of your essay, you will run the risk of losing your readers.

One introduction that answers these questions comes from an article by Roger Gibbins and Loleen Berdall entitled "The Roots of Western Alienation." After a brief outline of the alienation that western Canadians often feel from the rest of Canada, the authors turn to the connection between this alienation and the economy:

> Regional discontent is not an abstract concern but rather one that relates directly to the strategic positioning of the region within the new global (and continental) economy. Of necessity, this positioning takes place in part through the national economy and political system. Many of the West's linkages to the global economy are shaped by policies of the federal government; thus, how the West is treated nationally bears directly on its competitive position globally. This was particularly so in the past when the federal government set tariffs, provided the policy framework and much of the funding for a national transportation system, and established the immigration policies that settled the West. While the regional impact of federal policy has weakened in an era of progressive globalization—trade policy, for example, is now largely set within the context of the North American Free Trade Agreement (NAFTA) and the World Trade Organization (WTO) if not unilaterally by the United States—national policies still have significant, albeit diminished, impact on the global positioning of western Canada. As a consequence, debates about the place of the West within the broader Canadian community are much more than a rehashing of past grievances; they are debates about future aspirations, about challenges and policy capacity in fluid continental and global environments, about the prospects for regional prosperity. Therefore, understanding regional discontent is as much about unlocking the future as it is about unlocking the past.[45]

The authors start by emphasizing the immediate, practical, real-world importance of Western alienation. This should catch the attention of anyone who is interested in the economic health not just of the West but of Canada as a whole. They follow up by placing modern Western alienation in its historical context. Anyone who has wondered about the relevance of history to modern-day political and economic issues should be interested in reading this article. Finally, and still in the introductory section, Gibbins and Berdall connect the past not only to the present but to the future, reinforcing the urgency of understanding the West's discontent.

Implicitly, Gibbins and Berdall argue that historical perspectives inform the modern debate on the role of the West in Canada. They are not trying to attack or defend anyone, but rather to drive home the necessity, for policy-makers, of historical knowledge. They start to build their case very quickly by telling their audience why they should be interested, how future prosperity might be affected by past decisions and present policies, and why it is in Canada's interest to address regional discontent.

BUILD YOUR ESSAY WITH GOOD PARAGRAPHS

A paragraph is much more than an indented block of text. It should contribute to the overall argument of the essay by presenting evidence and developing inferences based on it. The best paragraphs have three components:

1. *A transition from the preceding paragraph.* Readers want to know why they are moving from one paragraph to the next. Good paragraphs are connected to each other with one or two **transition sentences**: signposts that remind readers where they have been and point to where they are going.

2. *A statement of the paragraph's point.* Each paragraph presents and develops a point that supports the overall argument of the essay.

3. *Supporting evidence.* What sort of evidence do you have to support that argument? Present the information from your sources that has allowed you to make historical inferences.

Of course there is no formula for combining these components. Sometimes the argument will be located in a transition sentence, and sometimes it will appear in its own "thesis sentence." Sometimes it will be presented before the evidence and sometimes after. The best historical writers blend transition, argument, and evidence so seamlessly that they carry the reader with them, progressively building their case as they move from one paragraph to the next.

Here is an example of paragraphing from a recent lower-division student paper on the history of British Columbia's Britannia Beach Mine:

Despite success, Britannia often underwent hardships, including disputes over the unionization of workers. In order to maintain fair wages and safe working conditions, in the mines, the workers staged numerous walkouts and strikes during Britannia's operation. Following the manager's death in 1906 and a drop in the copper market, concerns persisted about a lack of modernized machinery and whether profits could be obtained from low-grade ore. In response, the company hired John Moodie as general manager of the mines, and Moodie was given full power to institute his system of firm operational mining. Although he made substantial improvements to Britannia mines, expanded the workforce to almost 700 men, and developed the beach townsite, Moodie is most remembered for his firm attitude towards unions, alcohol, and worker insubordination. Failed attempts at unionization, were greeted with Moodie's directives to "pack up and [go] back to town," most notably with the Industrial Workers of the World in 1913 and the Western Federation of Miners in 1917. Being isolated and company-owned, Britannia allowed Moodie to enforce his zero tolerance rules. Over the next four decades Britannia workers would have to fight for unionization before it was agreed to by management. Their strikes represented the many difficulties that British Columbian workers in many different industries have had to endure.

In addition to labour disputes, Britannia also struggled through the adversity of numerous disasters including avalanches, fires and floods. In 1915, a mudslide consumed the Jane camp during the night, killing almost 60 sleeping men, women and children. In desperation, crews struggled by candlelight to dig out those buried beneath the debris and, to prevent another disaster, a second townsite was built further away, which eventually became known as Mt. Sheer. Furthermore, in 1918, Britannia was hit hard by a Spanish influenza epidemic that killed between forty and a hundred residents. . . . After each disaster, Britannia rebuilt and came together as a community to overcome such adversity.[46]

In this example, the first paragraph addresses difficulties in labour relations, particularly during the tenure of manager John Moodie, and the second extends the idea of "enduring difficulties" to encompass various "disasters." The first paragraph is summed up nicely in its last sentence. Then the second paragraph opens with a transition sentence that links the two sets of ideas.

DEFINE YOUR KEY TERMS EARLY

Never assume that your audience will understand important terms to mean the same thing that you do. Define your central concepts as soon as you introduce them, preferably at the beginning of your essay. You may find that you can use a definition as a springboard to discuss the complexities of your subject.

1. *Defining uncommon terms.* Sometimes you will need to define specialized or foreign terms that your audience might not recognize. In his 1995 lecture to the History of Science Society on the subject of Arabic science, A.I. Sabra discussed the role of the *muwaqqit*. What, you may wonder, is a *muwaqqit*? According to Sabra, a *muwaqqit* is a timekeeper in a mosque who uses astronomical methods to determine the exact timing of the five daily prayers. But when Sabra defines this term, he takes the opportunity to mention one of the distinctive features of Arabic science: "Through the introduction . . . of the office of *muwaqqit*, the timekeeper in charge of regulating the times of the five daily prayers, a place was created for the utilization of one form of scientific knowledge in a permanent religious

institution." Sabra defines the word in such a way that it leads readers to consider the larger issue of the relationship between religion and science.[47]

2. ***Redefining common terms.*** In addition to defining unfamiliar terms, sometimes you may need to redefine standard English words. This is exactly what William Cronon does in his book *Changes in the Land: Indians, Colonists, and the Ecology of New England*. The *Canadian Oxford Dictionary* defines "landscape" as "natural or imaginary scenery as seen in a broad view," but Cronon uses the word more broadly. Cronon's New Englanders saw that the "landscape was a visible confirmation of the state of human society."[48] An English landscape, a way of viewing and ordering the world, prevailed over an indigenous American landscape.

SET AN APPROPRIATE TONE

All writers must build a relationship with their readers. The best way to establish rapport is to find an appropriate, trustworthy tone.

1. Avoid the first person singular. Generally speaking, historians don't write in the first person singular. They recognize that personal biases enter historical writing—there is usually no need to overemphasize it. Therefore they rarely, if ever, make the personal angle explicit. You should follow their lead. If you have a statement to make—say, "Margaret Ormsby ignored the role of the First Nations in the development of British Columbian society"—don't preface it with "I think that" or "In my opinion." Just go ahead and make it. Readers will have no difficulty inferring that this is your opinion.

   In most cases, historians use the first person singular only when their personal experience is in some way relevant to their subject matter and they need to explain their relationship to it. Jean Barman's first-person approach in the article cited earlier in this chapter is one example of an appropriate use of the first person singular.

Similarly, Carl Degler begins his book *In Search of Human Nature*, about racial thinking in anthropology, as follows: "Like most white Americans of my sex and class (the son of a fireman) and my generation (born in 1921) I came into a world that soon made me a racist and a sexist."[49] He does this both to focus attention on his subject and to inform readers of his personal investment in it—a factor that they may wish to take into account when they evaluate his arguments.

2. ***Be judicious and dispassionate.*** All historians pass judgment on their subjects, but they usually try not to be too heavy-handed. For example, suppose you are writing about someone who is known to have committed a horrible crime. If the evidence speaks for itself, there is no need for you to make your judgment explicit: concentrate on presenting the facts and let readers form their own opinions.

Robert Jay Lifton is a psychiatrist and historian whose book *The Nazi Doctors* explores how it was possible for medical doctors such as Josef Mengele to serve the Nazi regime. Lifton outlines Mengele's well-known crimes—"selections, lethal injections, shootings, beatings, and other forms of deliberate killing"—in a matter-of-fact, dispassionate tone, with an occasional hint of irony. For example, he puts Mengele's experiments in the context of his medical career: "More than any other SS doctor, Mengele realized himself in Auschwitz. There he came into his own—found expression for his talents." Instead of condemning Mengele, Lifton presents him as the consummate clinical researcher, even in the midst of a concentration camp. Lifton's objective and ironic approach gives his argument—that Mengele had a schizoid personality and therefore was able to detach himself from the suffering he inflicted on others—a high degree of credibility.[50]

Sometimes it is enough just to describe a horrible event for your readers to understand that you find it repugnant. Afua Cooper begins her exploration of slavery in eighteenth-century Quebec as follows:

In April 1734, Montreal burned. A slave woman, Marie-Joseph Angélique, was the main suspect. She was arrested by the police and hauled in front of the court, and she endured a two-month trial. Throughout the trial, however, Angélique maintained her innocence. At the end of the ordeal, she was found guilty and condemned to be tortured, have her right hand cut off, and then be burned alive. Her sentence was appealed in the Conseil Supérieur, the highest court in the land, and the judges of the Conseil modified the grisly sentence—the slave woman was only to be tortured and then hanged.[51]

Cooper does not need to state that the trial and sentence were unjust. She does not overemphasize the vulnerability of the condemned woman or ridicule the Conseil Supérieur's concept of mercy. She makes her argument simply by recounting the facts, trusting that readers will find them as repugnant as she does.

TREAT OTHER WRITERS WITH CONSIDERATION

Scholarship thrives on lively debate and open disagreement, but it depends on mutual respect and careful consideration. When you write about other historians, give them the same respect that you would if you were speaking to them in person. Never oversimplify, misrepresent, or ridicule another historian's argument, no matter how strongly you may disagree, and never make personal attacks on opponents. You don't have to agree with them, but you must be polite and you must be fair.

ACCOUNT FOR COUNTERARGUMENTS

Don't just select one argument and then ignore all other possibilities. When you acknowledge the existence of alternative interpretations you increase the credibility and complexity of your own work. Your readers won't think you are weak; they will think you are fair. In fact, readers may already be aware of possible objections to your argument, or other sources that contradict it, and they will expect you to deal with them.

By the very nature of their work, historians know that no interpretation is flawless. In a short essay, it is often effective to note the main counter-arguments, and explain briefly why your argument remains more convincing. In a longer essay, thesis, or book, authors often address multiple counterarguments as they consider the evidence.

One example of counterargumentation can be found in Robert McElvaine's book *Eve's Seed: Biology, the Sexes, and the Course of History.* McElvaine reviews evidence from prehistory and evolutionary psychology suggesting that for most of human history, females were not necessarily subordinate to males. He argues that male domination is not natural, but can be explained historically as a by-product of the Agricultural Revolution, starting around 10,000 BCE. According to McElvaine, it was when men lost their roles as hunters that, out of insecurity and envy, they turned to misogyny.

To make this argument, McElvaine has to address two counterarguments: that human behaviour is completely determined by biology, and the opposite argument, that every individual is born with a clean slate, and that nurture is the determining factor.

McElvaine wants to demonstrate that both nature and nurture are important. First, he engages the two opposing positions with a joke. Quoting his own father in an early chapter title, he writes that people are "90 percent nature and 90 percent nurture." Next he moves to consider the "nurture" position:

> The reason that so many liberals have clung to their insistence that human nature should be ignored is . . . a fundamental misapprehension concerning the implications of human nature. They have feared that the admission of the existence of innate characteristics will lead to findings on how people *differ.* In fact, the real meaning of human nature, as [Franz] Boas understood, is to be found in showing the ways in which people are *alike.* As Robert Wright has said, unlike the old social Darwinists, "today's Darwinian anthropologists, in scanning the world's peoples, focus less on surface differences among cultures than on deep unities."

Now McElvaine turns to the "conservative" position advocated by "sociobiologists" such as Richard Dawkins and Edward Wilson, who believe that social behaviour is determined by Darwinian natural selection:

... Conservatives seize on the principle of natural selection to maintain that everything that exists should be left alone, because it was made that way by the god of adaptation. But this is not so. It ignores genetic drift, whereby characteristics come into being that provide no evolutionary advantage, but also no disadvantage, and so survive despite Darwinian selection, not because of it. The actual essence of the Darwinian principle of selection is not that a trait must be well adapted in order to survive, but that it not be *poorly* adapted relative to other traits. It is possible for some features to continue to develop after they have fulfilled their original evolutionary function. Human intellectual ability is probably an example of this. It grew far beyond what was necessary for human survival in the eons during which it was physically developing (although perhaps not beyond or even up to what is necessary for survival in the nuclear age; indeed it may yet prove to be ultimately maladaptive by destroying the species).

McElvaine's summary of the liberal and conservative positions is balanced and fair-minded, even though he strongly disagrees with both. By reporting accurately and engaging opposing arguments, he makes it more likely that liberals and conservatives alike will be persuaded to consider his argument: that liberal views on social and gender equality are actually supported by biological evidence.[52]

LEAD YOUR READERS TO AN INTERESTING CONCLUSION

Over the course of your essay, all your detailed evidence and analysis should serve to reinforce your main argument. By the time you reach your concluding paragraph, your readers will be ready for you to put your ideas back into a broader context.

There is no formula for a concluding paragraph. Even so, there are certain expectations. First, a conclusion ought to address the "Who cares?" question once again. How are your findings significant? How might they change the way the readers think?

Second, a conclusion should not simply repeat the introduction. If the essay has truly developed its central idea, there should be an interesting new way to sum it up.

One example of an interesting conclusion can be found in Mercedes Steedman's article "The Red Petticoat Brigade," on RCMP surveillance of the Ladies' Auxiliary of the Mine, Mill and Smelter Workers Union of Sudbury, Ontario, in the Cold War era. Why would the RCMP spend decades monitoring an organization devoted as much to bake sales as to labour activism? Steedman concludes that the surveillance reflected contemporary fear of the perceived threats posed by communism, as well as post-war concern over the proper place of women in society:

> The RCMP surveillance of innocuous social groups was part of a larger social construction of Cold War culture, one that turned neighbour against neighbour and generated a general climate of suspicion. In this way RCMP surveillance served to constrain the character of working-class post-war activism for both men and women. For working-class women activists, these constraints of post-war "normalcy" meant that women who openly advocated women's equality and social justice were immediately suspect, even when they were holding tea parties. Yet Mine Mill women did actively promote a greater voice for women of the day. Through the auxiliary movement, working-class women worked for the cessation of weapons testing, for full disarmament, and for the creation of conditions that, as Dorothy McDonald reported, "would enable women to fulfill their roles in society, as mothers, workers, and citizens which includes the right to work, the protection of motherhood, equal rights with regards to marriage, children and property."[53]

Steedman summarizes her argument and then goes beyond it to suggest that the Mine Mill women were in fact early activists in what would later become known as the women's liberation movement.

৵৹ REVIEW ৫৶

1. Be prepared to write several drafts.
2. Explain your purpose clearly.
3. Structure your argument carefully.
4. Define your terms.
5. Deal with counterarguments.
6. Make your conclusion count.

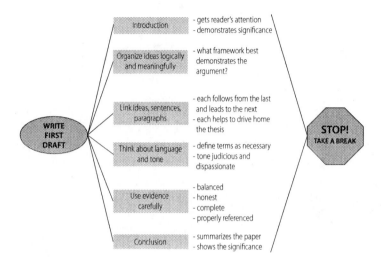

WRITE FIRST DRAFT

Introduction
- gets reader's attention
- demonstrates significance

Organize ideas logically and meaningfully
- what framework best demonstrates the argument?

Link ideas, sentences, paragraphs
- each follows from the last and leads to the next
- each helps to drive home the thesis

Think about language and tone
- define terms as necessary
- tone judicious and dispassionate

Use evidence carefully
- balanced
- honest
- complete
- properly referenced

Conclusion
- summarizes the paper
- shows the significance

STOP! TAKE A BREAK

∽ CHAPTER 7 ∾

NARRATIVE TECHNIQUES

You may decide to organize your essay either as one long narrative or as a series of short narratives illustrating particular points of analysis. Narrative structure is important in either case.

TELL A STORY

Every narrative has some easily recognized features: a narrator, one or more characters, a setting, and a plot that unfolds chronologically, over time. Historical narratives share these features with other forms of storytelling, including novels and epic poems.

One of the first historical narratives was written in the fifth century BCE by a Greek adventurer and storyteller named Herodotus. He used dramatic tension and colourful description to help his readers imagine the past. When he came to recount how the emperor Xerxes and his army destroyed the small contingent of Spartans guarding the pass at Thermopylae, he did not simply say that the outnumbered Spartans were brave and fought to the death. Instead he told how the Spartans responded when the massive Persian forces came into sight, not fleeing but calmly continuing to comb their long hair in preparation for battle. He also reported an anecdote told of a Spartan soldier named Dieneces:

> It is said before the battle he was told by a native of Trachis that, when the Persians shot their arrows, there were so many of them that they hid the sun. Dieneces, however, quite unmoved by the thought of the strength of the Persian army, merely remarked: "This is pleasant news . . . if the Persians hide the sun, we shall have our battle in the shade."[54]

WRITE A NARRATIVE TO SUPPORT AN ARGUMENT

Herodotus was not merely telling a story about a particular battle. He was selecting anecdotes and stories in order to build an argument for a particular interpretation of the event. The best storytellers are able to wrap a powerful argument in a seamless narrative. Herodotus told the story of Thermopylae because he wanted to persuade the Athenians that the Spartans had fought bravely in defence of a united Greece. He also wanted to illustrate the superiority of the Greeks, who were willing to die for their liberty, and the Persians, who had to whip their troops to make them fight.[55]

CHRONOLOGY AND CAUSATION

A historical narrative uses time to give structure to the past. For this reason, narratives have some obvious chronological features: a beginning, a middle, and an end. This may seem simple, but in the hands of a skilled historian a narrative's events do not simply follow one another: early events are related in some way to subsequent events.

If you are crafting a narrative, your first task will be to place important events in chronological order. This is vital to understanding the causes of things, and it is not as easy as you might think. For example, historians writing about the Crusades draw on accounts by both Muslims and Christians. Unfortunately, the two religious traditions follow different calendars, which means that the dates of one must be translated in order to establish a coherent chronology.

If you don't know the actual date of an event, you will have to find another source that will give you the information you need to place it in relation to another event. Eighteenth-century English parish records, for instance, don't give birth dates—only the dates when children were baptized. If you want to establish an individual's date of birth, you will have to find another source of information on the customs of that particular place in that particular period, one that will tell you how long after birth children were typically baptized. Establishing a chronology is not just an exercise: it helps you to understand change over time.

GET A SENSE OF CHANGE AND CONTINUITY

When you have established the sequence of events, you will begin to get a sense of how some things changed over time while others remained the same. Which events were entirely predictable in the context of the times? Which events were unexpected? Might different historical actors have had different perspectives on the same events?

In 1833, the British Parliament passed legislation abolishing the slave trade and calling for the emancipation of all colonial slaves as of 1 August 1834. After more than thirty years of abolitionist activism, a London journalist might have seen the abolition of slavery as inevitable. For a Barbadian slave, however, emancipation very likely came as a dramatic surprise. On the other hand, the change in the conditions of life for the latter might not have been dramatic at all. Throughout the Caribbean, former slaves were not released immediately: they remained bound to their former owners as apprentices for varying lengths of time. And once the apprenticeship phase had run its course, the land and capital required for sugar production remained out of reach for most, if not all, former slaves. Thus many had no choice but to continue working for their former owners. In that respect, then, former slaves might have experienced more continuity than change.[56]

SELECT THE PARTICIPANTS YOU WANT TO FOCUS ON

If you were telling a narrative of emancipation in Barbados, you could focus on former slaves and masters. Or you could choose a narrower focus: slave women who became entrepreneurs, or previously freed townsmen, or colonial bankers, or government officials. Don't forget that your story must make an argument. Do certain individuals illustrate your argument better than others? Were some people more significant agents of change than others? You might decide to exclude some people from your narrative altogether, or leave them in the background and bring others to the front of the stage.

FIND YOUR OWN VOICE AS A NARRATOR

It may take you some time and experimentation to discover your own
narrative voice. Every historian does this differently, but one rule always
applies: every narrator must be as faithful as possible to the people and
events of the past.

1.   *The omniscient narrator.* Some historians choose to remain
     in the background and tell their story from the perspective of
     an omniscient outsider. Christopher Hibbert uses this style of
     narration in his account of India's anticolonial rebellion of 1857,
     The Great Mutiny. Here he retells a famous story according to
     which the rebellion began when the British introduced a new
     paper gunpowder cartridge, greased with animal fat, that
     Muslim and Hindu troops would have to tear open using their
     teeth:

     > One day in January 1857 a low-caste labourer at Dum-Dum asked
     > a sepoy for a drink of water from his *lota*. The sepoy, being a
     > Brahmin, had naturally refused: his caste would not allow him to
     > grant such a request; he had just scoured his *lota*; the man would
     > defile it by his touch. "You will soon lose your caste altogether,"
     > the labourer told him. "For the Europeans are going to make you
     > bite cartridges soaked in cow and pork fat. And then where will
     > your caste be?"[57]

2. *The uncertain narrator.* Not all historians approve of omniscient
     narration, however, and not all sources are reliable enough to
     permit it. (In fact, the origins of the 1857 rebellion itself are still
     the subject of controversy.) When source materials are so scarce
     or ambiguous that speculation is required to fill in the gaps, it's
     best to make those limitations explicit to readers from the start.
     John Demos uses this strategy in his book *The Unredeemed
     Captive*: the story of Eunice Williams, a child who was captured
     by Mohawks in the Deerfield Massacre of 1704. After her abduc-
     tion, Eunice adapted to the ways of the Kahnawake Iroquois.
     This disturbed her family but it did not stop them from trying
     to bring her back to Massachusetts. The information available

to Demos was extremely limited, consisting mainly of the letters and diaries of Eunice's English relatives. The family spent decades trying to learn about Eunice, but in the end they recorded very little information. Demos struggles to extract meaning from these scarce sources, but his narrative is at its most compelling when he incorporates quotations from them into his text:

> Different it [Eunice's new "style of life"] was, very different. And yet, within a relatively short time, it took. By 1707, Eunice was reported to be "unwilling to return." And the Indians— including, one would presume, her new family—"would as soon part with their hearts" as with this successfully "planted" child.[58]

CHOOSE YOUR OWN BEGINNING AND END

In real life, events are so interconnected across chronological and geographical boundaries that it may be impossible to identify either a beginning or an end. Yet every narrative must have both. Hibbert begins his story of the 1857 rebellion with a description of a typical working day for Sir Thomas Metcalfe, British representative to the king of Delhi:

> He returned from his office at half past two for dinner at three. After dinner he sat reading for a time before going down to the billiard-room. A game of billiards was followed by two hours spent on the terrace contemplating the river. Then it was time for a light supper and an evening hookah. Immediately the clock struck eight, he stood up and went to bed, undoing his neckcloth and throwing it, together with his well-tailored coat, on to the floor to be picked up by the appropriate servant. If this or any other servant did not perform his duties to the master's entire satisfaction, Sir Thomas would send for a pair of white kid gloves which were presented to him on a silver salver. These he would draw on with becoming dignity, then firmly pinch the culprit's ear.[59]

Hibbert is not simply telling a story about an indolent, autocratic colonial official. He is setting the scene for a much larger story about how Indians rebelled against British authority, how the British forces crushed the rebels, and how this experience transformed both South Asia and the British Empire.

Hibbert sets his the opening scene in Delhi because that is where his narrative will reach its climax, when the British recapture the city. Similarly, although the rebellion ended in different ways and different places for different people, his narrative ends when the British banish the king of Delhi:

> The trial lasted more than two months; but the verdict was never in doubt. On 29 March [the king] was found guilty on all charges and later sentenced to be transported for life to Rangoon. He left Delhi in October accompanied by Jawan Bakht, another young son whom he had had by a concubine, and by a most unwilling Zinat Mahal who, by now "quite tired of him," described him as a "troublesome, nasty, cross old fellow." He died on 7 November 1862 in Rangoon where the descendants of his son, Jawan Bakht, are still living today.[60]

In choosing to conclude his narrative at this point, Hibbert brings the story that began in Delhi full circle. In addition, the exile of the king of Delhi draws at least two strands of the story together: a dispute over who would succeed the king had been a contributing cause of the rebellion; and much of the fighting had taken place in and around Delhi. Furthermore, by referring to the king's descendants, Hibbert is able to emphasize the enduring legacy of the rebellion. Keep his example in mind when you are constructing a historical narrative: choose a beginning and an end that suit the story you want to tell and the argument you want to make.

∽ REVIEW ∾

1. Use anecdotes to make deliberate points.
2. Include causes and consequences.
3. Control your materials: pick the characters and events you need to make your argument.

∾ CHAPTER 8 ∾

WRITING SENTENCES

Historians, like all writers, want to communicate their ideas effectively. They differ from other writers, however, in some of the conventions they follow to achieve this goal. The differences can be confusing for writers trained in other disciplines. But no historical convention is arbitrary: all of them help to ensure that historians' representations of the past are as faithful as possible.

CHOOSE PRECISE VERBS

At the heart of the sentence is the verb that carries the action. Precise verbs are virtually always preferable to vague ones. What is a vague verb? The most common is the verb "to be"—"is," "are," "was," and so on. These words are indispensable, as the last few sentences show. But beginning writers tend to overuse them—a habit that makes for a dull, lifeless style. It's true that "Alexander Graham Bell was the inventor of the telephone." But you could make the same point more directly if you used the verb that corresponds to the noun "inventor." "Alexander Graham Bell invented the telephone" is more succinct and sounds more lively and natural. In the same way, you could write "There was a large crowd at the meeting," but "A large crowd attended the meeting" sounds better. If you find yourself using a verb of being, try to think of a more precise, active alternative.

MAKE PASSIVE SENTENCES ACTIVE

One of the main goals of historical writing is to uncover who did what. It follows that one of the worst things a historian can do is to obscure that information. Too often, that is exactly what the passive voice does. In fact, passive constructions can obliterate historical actors altogether:

"New France was surrendered in September 1760." By whom? To whom? If you can't state with certainty that "Governor Vaudreuil surrendered New France to General Amherst in September 1760," then you owe your readers an explanation.

As you read more history, you may notice that the passive is often a sign of weak reasoning or insufficient information. This is not necessarily the case in other disciplines. Until quite recently, for instance, use of the passive was standard in the natural sciences, which sought to downplay individuals' personal involvement in research and emphasize the objectivity of their work. One of the biggest challenges for historians of science today is to cut through the passive prose and find out not just what was done, but who did it.

There are times when the passive can't be avoided. In some circumstances it is even appropriate: the preceding sentence would have been less direct if it had read 'There are times when historians can't avoid using the passive." The best writers will often use one or two passive constructions per page. Nevertheless, the passive can confuse the order of ideas and should be used sparingly.

USE THE PAST TENSE

Historians rarely write in the present tense. This is hardly surprising. If you are discussing events that took place in the past, it makes sense to use the past tense. It also helps to ensure that you keep those events in an intelligible chronological order.

It is conventional for scholars of literature to write about authors and their works in the present tense. Thus a literary critic discussing the work of the novelist Richard Wright might write that "Wright speaks eloquently and forcefully against American racism and capitalism," and a literature instructor would probably use the present tense when discussing Wright's use of language. By contrast, a historian analyzing Wright's work—perhaps as a way to understand the time in which he was writing—would use the past tense to discuss the author himself: "Born in Mississippi in 1908, Wright moved to Chicago in 1927 and joined the American Communist party there in 1932, at the height of the Great Depression." Using the present tense might confuse the chronology of Wright's life and times, but using the past tense makes it possible to locate events clearly in relationship to one another.

The present tense is appropriate, however—even for a historian—when discussing fictional characters or events. Similarly, historians use the present tense when writing about contemporary work or living scholars.

Try to avoid split infinitives

In English, the infinitive is the form of the verb accompanied by the preposition "to," as in "to go," "to walk," or "to be or not to be." It is the most basic form, unattached to any subject or object.

For generations, teachers insisted that the infinitive should never be "split" by placing an adverb between "to" and the verb, as in the famous Star Trek line "To boldly go where no man has gone before." Today most grammarians agree that split infinitives are very common in spoken English, and that there are times when placing the adverb anywhere else would alter the meaning of the sentence. There are also times when a split infinitive simply sounds better. If the Star Trek writers had put their adverb in the "correct" place, the line would have been "To go boldly. . . ." How uninspiring.

In general, though, historians still try to avoid splitting infinitives, if only because so many people consider it a serious grammatical error. If repositioning the adverb would change your meaning or create an awkward, unnatural rhythm, you may be able to recast the sentence.

Write complete sentences

In principle, a sentence is a sentence only if it has both a subject (noun) and a predicate (verb). And yet there are times when a phrase with neither can be appropriate (as in the case of the "How uninspiring" comment above). Incomplete sentences can add punch and colour to informal writing, but they really do not have a place in formal historical writing. If you do use an incomplete sentence in a work of history, you should be very sure that readers will understand your intent: otherwise they will simply assume that your grammar is not up to scratch.

PUT YOUR IDEAS IN AN INTELLIGIBLE ORDER

You must put your ideas in an order that your readers will understand. This is not as easy as it sounds. After weeks of reading and research, you will have become so steeped in your topic that the complex connections between the people, ideas, and events you are writing about will seem perfectly obvious to you. Now it is your job to unravel those complexities and place your ideas in a sequence of words. In each sentence, you must imagine what your readers need to know first, second, and third. Reread every sentence you write and ask yourself whether it would be totally clear to someone else. Unless your professor instructs you otherwise, you should assume that you're writing for an intelligent reader who is generally well informed, but has no specific knowledge of your topic area.

KEEP RELATED WORDS TOGETHER

"The tail-gunner saw a cloud form over Hiroshima in the shape of a mushroom": this sentence likely makes perfect sense to you because you have seen pictures of the infamous mushroom cloud. Imagine, though, if you spoke that sentence to someone who had never seen such a picture. That person would have to rely on the sequence of the words to grasp your meaning, and in this case the sequence would be baffling. After all, it isn't Hiroshima that has the shape of the mushroom: it's the cloud. Your point would be clearer if you kept related words close together: "The tail-gunner saw a mushroom-shaped cloud form over Hiroshima." If you keep related words together, readers won't have to pause at the end of the sentence to figure out what it meant.

MAKE SURE THAT PRONOUN REFERENCES ARE CLEAR

By definition, a pronoun substitutes for a noun. For a pronoun to make sense, however, readers have to be able to tell which noun it replaces, and they can't do that unless you have taken care to avoid any possible ambiguity. You know in your head which pronoun refers to which noun, but your readers must infer the relationship from the way you place the words. Consider this sentence: "John A. Macdonald's 1864 partner-ship with George Brown demonstrated his political practicality and flexibility." Does "his" refer to Macdonald or to Brown? A reader might infer that, since "his" is closer to "Brown," the practicality and flexibility are his. But this may not be your meaning. Both Brown and Macdonald were talented politicians, and both could be described as practical and flexible. There are several ways of recasting the sentence to avoid such confusion: "John A. Macdonald demonstrated political practicality and flexibility in his 1864 partnership with George Brown" or "John A. Macdonald's 1864 partnership with George Brown demonstrated his own political practicality and flexibility"; or even "John A. Macdonald's 1864 partnership with George Brown demonstrated Brown's political practicality and flexibility." In each case, a minor adjustment will create a much clearer sentence.

KEEP SUBJECTS AND VERBS CLOSE TOGETHER

The principal relationship in a sentence is between the subject and the verb. In general, it's best not to put too much information between them. Take a look at this sentence: "Grey Owl, after two years with the Canadian army in the First World War, spent his life as a hunter, guide, and conservationist." As a reader, you have to hold "Grey Owl" in the back of your mind until you find out what he is doing. The idea would be clearer if you wrote that "After two years with the Canadian army in the First World War, Grey Owl spent his life as a hunter, guide, and conservationist." It's usually acceptable to place a short phrase between a subject and verb, however: "Grey Owl, born Archie Belaney, spent his life as a hunter, guide, and conservationist."

BEGIN ON COMMON GROUND AND MOVE TOWARDS A NEW POINT

A sentence is not just a series of words arranged in an orderly fashion. In history, as in all writing, a sentence develops an idea that has already been established (usually, though not necessarily, in the preceding sentence) and develops it so as to carry the reader in a certain direction.

In other words, a sentence does not function in isolation: it needs to connect in some way with the sentences on either side of it. Consider this sequence of sentences:

> Mackenzie King was particularly devoted to his dog Pat I. He had three Irish terriers, all of which were named Pat. After Pat I died, King tried to communicate with his spirit.

Here the reader has to jump from a specific statement about one of King's dogs to a general statement about all of them and then back to another specific statement. A better sequence would move from the general to the specific:

> Mackenzie King had three Irish terriers, all of which were named Pat. He was particularly devoted to Pat I. After Pat I died, King tried to communicate with his spirit.

In this sequence, the connections between the sentences are smooth.

PUT THE EMPHASIS AT THE END

If you are developing your ideas over the course of a sentence, then the end of the sentence should be interesting and emphatic. One master of emphatic writing (and speaking) was Winston Churchill. Here is what Churchill wrote about the Crusades in his book *The Birth of Britain*:

> The Crusading spirit had for some time stirred the minds of men all over western Europe. The Christian kingdoms of Spain had led the way with their holy wars against the Arabs. Now, towards the end of the eleventh century, a new enemy of Christendom appeared fifteen hundred miles to the east. The Seljuk Turks were pressing hard upon the Byzantine Empire in Asia Minor, and harassing devout pilgrims from Europe through Syria to the Holy Land.[61]

Notice how each sentence begins with a connection to the previous sentence. Also notice how each sentence develops in a new direction and concludes with a new idea. The second sentence is especially skillful. It begins by saying something specific about the western European

Christians, but then leads readers to consider the Christians' enemies, the Arabs.

USE PARALLEL FORMS FOR EMPHASIS

One of the best tricks for writing an effective sentence is to use a parallel construction, expressing related ideas in a similar grammatical form. On 8 October 1940, as Nazi bombers were pounding Britain, Churchill told the House of Commons that "Death and sorrow will be the companions of our journey; hardship our garment; constancy and valour our only shield. We must be united, we must be undaunted, we must be inflexible."[62] He constructed the first sentence loosely around the repetition of "our"; then he constructed the second sentence tightly around the repetition of "we must be." In a parallel construction, parallel ideas are expressed in a parallel grammatical structure.

BREAK THE RULES IF YOU MUST

As valuable as all these conventions may be, there are times when strict observance could force you to write an ugly, unnatural sentence. In such cases, break the rules. Good historical writers understand the spirit of the law as well as the letter. Your first task is to get your meaning across, and to do it persuasively.

✍ REVIEW ✍
1. Think! Make every sentence count.
2. Pay special attention to verbs.
3. Use word order to your advantage.

ꙮ **CHAPTER 9** ꙮ

CHOOSING WORDS

In history as in life, word choice can make all the difference. The past abounds with catastrophic examples of poorly chosen words. One example is the 1840 Treaty of Waitangi, in which the British took New Zealand from the Maoris by mistranslating the word for "sovereignty."[63] This deliberate act of imprecision has caused a century and a half of bad feelings. Get into the habit of checking your essays for diction. The basic rules of diction often strike inexperienced writers as arbitrary. They are not.

BE CONCISE

Some people seem to think that the best way to impress readers with the complexity of their ideas is to use as many words as possible to express them. They are wrong. Readers will be more impressed if you make every word count. If "It is an undeniable fact that William the Conqueror was instrumental in establishing the Norman regime," why not simply state the fact? "William the Conqueror established the Norman regime." Why use sixteen words to say something that you could say in seven? If you can resist the temptation to cram your paper with unnecessary words, readers will thank you for not straining their patience.

AVOID JARGON

Most historians try to use language that non-specialist readers will understand. This tendency sets history apart from several of its fellow social sciences. Disciplines such as anthropology, economics, political science, and sociology each have their own **jargon**: a specialized language that helps people within the field communicate but tends to shut everyone else out. History doesn't have its own private language, but sometimes historians will borrow jargon from other fields. For example, the *Canadian Oxford Dictionary* defines "hegemony" as "leadership esp. by one state of a confederacy," but professional historians associate the term with a Marxist philosopher and political theorist named Antonio Gramsci, who used it in the sense of social power or dominance. If you are writing for historians, you can expect them to understand the term as you do, but to a wider audience "hegemony" may be incomprehensible jargon. When in doubt, either use ordinary language or be sure to define your terms carefully.

Awkward jargon can also slip into historical writing from the legal profession. Legal documents are written for a specific audience (the court), and purpose (to protect the interests of the lawyer's client). Lawyers use archaic terminology, repetition, and formal terms like "the said," "party to the first part," and "stipulate." This kind of language should be used only by lawyers, for lawyers. It has no place in a history paper, unless you are writing about an actual court case and need to quote from the proceedings. Otherwise, use plain English.

Perhaps even less appropriate for historical writing is government jargon, sometimes known as "officialese." This is the awkward, abstract, often pompous language that many politicians and bureaucrats learn to use to protect themselves, avoid precise commitments, or make themselves sound important. In his famous essay "Politics and the English Language," George Orwell imagined how a bureaucrat might translate the following passage from the Bible (*Ecclesiastes* 9:11):

> I returned and saw under the sun, that the race is not to the swift, nor the battle to the strong, neither yet bread to the wise, nor yet riches to men of understanding, nor yet favour to men of skill; but time and chance happeneth to them all.

Here is Orwell's translation:

> Objective consideration of contemporary phenomena compels the conclusion that success or failure in competitive activities exhibits no tendency to be commensurate with innate capacity, but that a considerable element of the unpredictable must invariably be taken into account.[64]

Orwell's point is clear: the pretentious, abstract language of the bureaucratic "translation" is no match for the clean, simple words, natural rhythms, and concrete imagery of the original passage.

AVOID PRETENTIOUS LANGUAGE

Don't count on big, complicated words to make you look smart or sound appropriately formal. You may only wind up confusing and annoying your readers. You may want to argue that central planning had a "procrustean" effect on Soviet engineering, but if your readers don't know that the word refers to a ruthless insistence on uniformity, you won't gain much ground with them. Even if they do know the word, it's likely to stand out from the rest of your writing and sound out of place. Control the urge to show off: use only words that you are comfortable with.

AVOID COLLOQUIAL LANGUAGE

Most history instructors will expect you to write in formal English. This means that you should avoid slang, contractions (isn't, doesn't, it's), and an overly casual tone, except as part of a quotation. Such informal or **colloquial language** is fine in many other types of writing (such as this guide), but it does not belong in formal academic writing.

BE SENSITIVE TO POLITICAL ISSUES

Historical writing has always reflected the politics of the times. Today historians are particularly sensitive to language that could be perceived as discriminatory or "politically incorrect." Conservatives may complain that liberals are forcing "linguistic engineering" on them; liberals, that conservatives have not gone far enough to purge their language of words that may cause offence. The dispute will never be resolved, but everyone can agree that writers who want to communicate need to be aware of how their readers will respond to their language.

Racial designations in particular have changed considerably over recent decades. "Negro" and "coloured" changed to "black" and then "black" was increasingly replaced by "African-American," "African-Canadian," and so on.

In Canada, "Indian" has been largely replaced by "First Nations" in the case of organized bands or communities, although "Indian" is still required in some legal contexts. In broader contexts, especially those that include Métis and Inuit people, "Aboriginal" and "Native" are fine so long as you use them as adjectives (as in "Aboriginal people" or "Native traditions"), but they should not be used as nouns. If you are writing about a particular group, nation, or band (a unit of administration), you should always use its specific name. You should also be aware that modern terms and classifications do not necessarily coincide with historic realities. Some First Nations people, for example, point out that the concept of the "nation" itself is not indigenous to their societies: it is a European concept that was introduced to them relatively recently. Finally, note that what is considered "correct" in terms of titles and spellings may be a subject of debate: try to be informed about such debates and sensitive to them. Whenever possible, call people by the names they call themselves.

BE SENSITIVE TO GENDER ISSUES

In the 1890s Oscar Wilde said, "Anybody can make history. Only a great man can write it." His point was to call attention to the challenge of writing history well, but people today could be forgiven if they were distracted from it by the apparent sexism of the phrase "great man." It's quite possible that Wilde had no intention of ruling out the idea of a great woman historian. But he was a man of his time, and at that time "man" meant (among other things) "human" or "person."

In recent years historians have become more sensitive to gender. This is reflected not only in their intellectual interests but also in their historical writing. Years ago it was acceptable to say, for example, "The historian must analyze sources. He must understand the relevant documents." The use of the masculine pronoun to refer to a noun of indeterminate gender was conventional. Fortunately, there are plenty of female historians today—so many that Wilde's statement now seems not only biased but inaccurate.

To avoid such sexist pitfalls, you may be tempted to use keyboard gymnastics: "He/she must understand the relevant documents," or, even worse, "S/he must understand. . . ." Slashed pronouns are usually easy to avoid. First, consider using neutral pronouns like "everyone," "anybody," and "everybody." If that doesn't work, you can often turn a singular into a plural: "Historians must analyze sources. They must understand the relevant documents." Changing a gender-specific singular to a gender-neutral plural conveys the same idea without any sexist overtones.

You might also be tempted to substitute the third-person-singular neutral pronoun "one" for a gender-biased "he." "When one is a historian, one must analyze sources." This construction is grammatically correct, but it almost always sounds pretentious today.

While we are on the subject of gender-neutral language, it's worth noting one other common problem: the word "mankind." An easy way around this one is simply to substitute "people" or "humankind," whichever suits your meaning more precisely.

Avoid euphemisms

"Politically correct" language is sometimes necessary to avoid giving offence, but it can often seem silly or evasive, if not downright deceitful. If you describe people you believe to be stupid as "intellectually challenged," you are using a **euphemism:** a polite term designed to disguise a harsh reality. The twentieth century seems to have been especially rich in euphemisms: torched villages were "pacified," totalitarian regimes were "people's republics," and the massacre of one ethnic group by another was a matter of "cleansing." In general, it's best to say what you really mean. It's also a good idea, when you come across a euphemism, to ask yourself whose interest it really serves.

Choose figurative language carefully

When you are writing about a subject that is likely to be unfamiliar to your readers, it often helps to make an imaginative comparison with something they know well—in other words, to use a simile or a metaphor. It would be perfectly acceptable to write "Simón Bolívar took part in the overthrow of Spanish rule in the Americas." It would be better to use a slightly more informative metaphor: "Simón Bolívar played a leading role in the overthrow of Spanish rule in the Americas." It might be even more effective to say that "Simón Bolívar was the George Washington of Spanish America," at least if you were writing for an American audience—although you might have to sustain the metaphor by specifying the respects in which they resembled one another. Metaphors and similes add colour to historical writing, but it takes practice to use them well.

USE METAPHORS AND SIMILES JUDICIOUSLY

There are several ways for a metaphor to go awry. Suppose, for instance, that you had described Bolívar as "the John Chilembwe of Spanish America." For one thing, chances are that most people reading an essay on Venezuelan history would never have heard of Chilembwe, a Baptist convert who led a rebellion against British colonial rule in Nyasaland (the future Malawi) in 1913. But the comparison is hopelessly flawed in any case because Chilembwe's revolution failed while Bolívar's succeeded. Metaphors and similes can add vitality to your writing, but only if they make sense to your readers.

AVOID CLICHÉS

Readers generally welcome colourful language, but they will find your colours boring if they are introduced for no particular reason or are too predictable. Colourful expressions that have been overused are called **clichés**. Replace them with plain language or less predictable metaphors.

There is a simple test you can use to spot a cliché. If you can remove the last word from a phrase and still be sure that readers will be able to fill it in, you are looking at a cliché:

- "Queen Elizabeth did not suffer fools . . . (gladly)."
- "Albert Einstein burned the midnight . . . (oil)."
- "The bubonic plague reared its ugly . . . (head)."

DON'T USE UNFAMILIAR FOREIGN WORDS

Historians often use foreign words or expressions. Some foreign terms have come into common English usage, as in "Trudeau was a politician *par excellence*," or "The right of *habeas corpus* is fundamental to Canadian law." When you write about a foreign culture, however, you should be careful with foreign terms.

The rule of thumb is to use only terms that your audience will understand. Imagine that you were writing about the history of the amaXhosa, a people of southern Africa. If the class were a seminar on southern African history and your instructor was a specialist in the field, it might well be appropriate for you to spell out the name "amaXhosa." This is because a specialist in southern African history would know that these people form the plural of their collective name by adding the prefix "ama." If you were writing for a more general audience—say, in a survey of world history—you probably wouldn't want to bother explaining the linguistic intricacies. In that case the best choice might be to refer to your subjects as "the Xhosa," a compromise that would let readers know you were savvy enough not to apply the English rule for forming plurals to a foreign word. It's important to know your readers and to meet them on common ground.

CHECK FOR COMMON DICTION PROBLEMS

It's easy to misuse words and expressions, especially ones that are often misused or misunderstood. If you suspect that you may have misused one of the following words or phrases in an essay, run a search on your computer to find it. Then consult your dictionary to make sure you have used it correctly.

If you need further assistance on points of usage, ask a reference librarian to help you find *The New Fowler's Modern English Usage*, ed. R.W. Burchfield (Oxford: Oxford University Press, 1996). The updated version of H.W. Fowler's classic work on English usage, it is the basis for many of the entries in the following list of common problems in historical writing:

AD and **BC** are abbreviations meaning *Anno domini* ("the year of our Lord") and "Before Christ." Increasingly, they are being replaced by the non-religious abbreviations BCE and CE, meaning "Before Common Era" and " Common Era" respectively. When you think about it, though, the new abbreviations don't really change anything.

Accept and **except** have very different meanings. "Accept" is a verb that means to receive or agree to something, while "except" is a preposition indicating that something is excluded or omitted. To keep the words separate in your mind, you might find it helpful to link *ex*cept with *ex*clude.

Affect and **effect** confuse many students, but they are quite easy to differentiate. "Affect" is most often used as a verb meaning "to act upon": for example, hunger might affect one's mood. "Effect," on the other hand, is usually a noun referring to a result: one effect of a bad mood might be that you snap at your roommate.

All right is proper for formal writing. Many people spell it as "alright," but most authorities regard "alright" as overly casual. It's not all right to write "alright" in a formal essay.

And/or appears frequently in insecure writing, possibly because it has a legalistic sound to it. "And/or" is not incorrect, but it is awkward and usually unnecessary. You can avoid it by substituting "X or Y or both" or even a simple "or."

Ante- and **anti-** are two Latin prefixes that students often confuse. "Ante" means *before*, while "anti" means *against*. For example, "antebellum America" refers to the period before the American Civil War, whereas "antiwar protestors" opposed the war.

Because is a common word in historical writing, because historians are often seeking to explain what caused something to happen: "Letitia Youmans founded the first Canadian local of the Women's Christian Temperance Union because she was distressed by the effects of alcohol on family life." Elementary-school teachers tell students not to start a sentence with "because," and in general they are right to do so. "Because" introduces a clause that depends on another clause; if you reversed the order of the two clauses about Youmans, the sentence would be harder to follow. You need to know the effect (that is, what has happened) before you can really take in the cause (the reason why). Still, there are circumstances when it is reasonable to make an exception to the rule.

Cannot is usually written as one word, not two ("can not"). "Can't" is a contraction, inappropriate in academic writing.

Different is the subject of some debate. Real sticklers will tell you that "different" can be followed only by "from," never by "than" or "to." The editors of the *Oxford English Dictionary* disagree. They say that people have been using "different to" since 1526 and "different than" since 1644. Is it possible that so many people could be so wrong for so long? Perhaps. Somehow, "different from" still sounds better.

Double negatives are not uncommon in historical writing, but they should be used sparingly. Two negatives always cancel each other out: "John A. MacDonald was not displeased by the result of the vote" is a roundabout way of saying that he *was* pleased. Occasionally a double negative can add an ironic note (as in the first sentence above), but a straightforward positive is usually best.

Due to might seem harmless enough, but generations of history professors have warned students against it. Strunk and White, in their classic *The Elements of Style*, explain that "due to" should be used only to mean "attributable to," as in "Custer's defeat was due to poor intelligence." It should not substitute for "because" or "through," as in "Custer lost the battle due to poor intelligence."

Into and **in to** are not interchangeable. "Into" is the word you want when you are talking about motion ("She walked into the meeting"), direction ("He looked into her eyes"), or a change of condition or state: ("A caterpillar turns into a butterfly"; "The group separated into factions"; "The marchers broke into song"). Sometimes, however, "in" and "to" are completely separate. For example, in the sentence "The troops moved in to surround the rebels," the "in" is part of the verbal phrase "moved in," while the "to" is part of the infinitive "to surround." In other cases the "to" may be a simple preposition: "He turned the umbrella in to the lost and found."

It's and **its** get confused frequently, even though they mean two completely different things. "It's" is the contraction of "it is": "It's not too late to learn how to write history." "Its" is the possessive form of "it": "When Castro lit a Montecristo, its pungent smoke filled the air." (It's worth remembering that, since "it's" is a contraction, it should not appear in academic writing anyway.)

Led to. It may be true that the First World War led to the Second World War: just don't confuse chronology with causation. The events of 1939 certainly followed those of 1914, but does that mean that they were caused by them? "Led to" will lead your readers to expect an explanation of how the first war helped to cause the second.

Lie and **lay** cause a lot of trouble. Generally speaking, to "lie" in the physical sense means to lie down, as in "lie down on a bed." "Lay," on the other hand, means to place something, as in "lay down a heavy load." We lie down when we are tired, but first we lay down whatever we have been carrying. The confusion probably arises because "lay" is also the past tense of "lie" ("I lay down on the couch for a nap and two minutes later the phone rang").

Lifestyle is an imprecise modern term that has no place in historical writing. The following sentence comes from a student essay: "The lifestyle of the African-American slaves cannot be compared with the lifestyle of the concentration camp inmates." It's unlikely that either of those groups ever had a lifestyle. The writer would have done better to refer to their living conditions or their experiences.

Native is a dangerous word in historical writing. You could refer to "the native Tahitians" just as you might refer to "the native French." But you should never refer to either group as "the natives." "Natives" is a term that Europeans once reserved for people from other parts of the world whom they deemed to be uncivilized. Today that kind of derogatory language is not tolerated. By contrast, the adjective "Native" (with a capital "N") is widely accepted, along with "Aboriginal" (as long as it's capitalized and used as an adjective).

People is a deceptively simple word that is easy to misuse. It can refer to a group of human beings who share some characteristic: "Aboriginal people made up 3.8% of Canada's population in 2006." It can also refer to those who belong to a state or nation: "Aboriginal peoples such as the Cree and the Ojibway are struggling to preserve their languages." In the same way, we refer to the specific European peoples, such as the French or the Germans, and also to European people more generally.

Principal and **principle** can be quite confusing. Principal is an adjective that refers to the first or the most important: for example, the principal dancer in a ballet company, or the principal points of an argument. Principle, on the other hand, is a noun referring to a general law, a rule or a standard: for instance, the principle of equal pay for equal work.

Regard is misused frequently in expressions such as "with regards to" and "in regards to." There are two proper ways to use "regard." If it is a noun (part of a compound preposition), use the singular: "with regard to" or "in regard to." If it is a verb, conjugate accordingly: "as it regards" or "as they regard."

That and **which** have been the subject of considerable confusion among historians and other writers. In the following sentences, which one would you use?

1.   "The tariffs *that/which* came to be known as the Corn Laws were repealed in 1846.

2. "The Corn Laws, *that/which* had protected English farmers from foreign competition, were repealed in 1846."

If you chose *that* for sentence 1 and *which* for sentence 2, you probably already know the difference between "restrictive" and "non-restrictive modifiers." In the first sentence, the phrase "(*that/which*) came to be known as the Corn Laws" is restrictive (or "defining") because it is essential to identify the particular tariffs in question.

In the second sentence, by contrast, the phrase "which had protected English farmers from foreign competition" is non-restrictive: parenthetical information that is not essential to the meaning of the sentence and therefore is set off by commas. Consistent use of "that" for restrictive and "which" for non-restrictive modifiers does make for a cleaner style. But you may notice that many fine writers do not follow the rule.

There and **their.** "There" is the adverb ("He worked there for thirty years") and 'their" is the possessive pronoun ("She is their representative.") Here is a sentence to show the difference: "In his famous painting of the Fathers of Confederation, Robert Harris paid careful attention to their positioning so as to show that there was a real hierarchy of political importance among them."

To, **too,** and **two** also give many students trouble. The simple "to" is a preposition ("He decided to run for election"; "She was elected to the House of Commons"). "Too" is an adverb with several uses ("This coffee is too hot to drink now"; "Did your brother go too?"). And "two" is the number. They mean completely different things. Here is a sentence that makes the differences clear: "When they went to Montreal, they saw two hockey games and bought too many souvenirs."

Tribe and **tribal** are subject to the same general rules as "Native." A long time ago, anthropologists used "tribe" precisely to refer to a group of people who claim descent from a common ancestor, real or imagined. Unfortunately, some historians and journalists took to using "tribe" loosely and offensively, to refer to any group of people with brown skin. Even today, a conflict that would be described as "ethnic" if it took place in Bosnia is likely to be described as "tribal" if it takes place in Rwanda. This usages derives from efforts of European administrators to classify and regulate the peoples of their former colonies. Ironically, some African and Native American groups took up the practice and now call themselves "tribes."

Were and **where** seem to confuse many students. "Were" is a verb form and "where" is an adverb that usually refers to a place or a situation: "The *filles du roi* were the young Frenchwomen whose passage to Canada, where they hoped to find husbands, was sponsored by the king."

Whose and **who's**. "Whose" is the possessive form of the word "who" ("The politician whose speeches were most effective"), while "who's" is a contraction of "who is" ("The politician who's running in the next election.") Since it is not appropriate to use contractions in academic writing, it is surprising to see how often   "who's" turns up in student essays.

ᥱᴦ REVIEW ᥱᴧ
1. Choose your words carefully.
2. Spelling counts!
3. Avoid slang and contractions.
4. Be direct—say what you mean.

ᥱᴦ PRACTICE EXERCISE ᥱᴧ

For each of the following sentences, choose the correct word to fill the blank space.

1. When Amor de Cosmos entered BC politics, he attacked the ruling elites and (there/their) _____ privileges.
2. In Canada, conscription was used in (to/two/too) _____ twentieth-century world wars.
3. After a lengthy political debate, (that/which) _____ was quite heated, Canadians rejected the Charlottetown Constitutional Accord.
4. The Red River Resistance of 1869–70 (cannot/can not) _____ be seen as a complete success.

5. It is (all right/alright) _____ to ask questions about referencing methods.

6. In the 1860s, (there/their) _____ were several Fenian raids into Canadian territory.

7. In the 1960s, (ante/anti-) _____ war sentiment was quite strong in Canada.

8. The principal players in the Nootka Sound Convention of 1790 (were/where) _____ the British and Spanish governments.

9. The Bluenose schooner was first depicted on the dime in 1937, at the height of (its/it's) _____ fame.

10. The Winnipeg General Strike of 1919 had an impact (that/which) _____ was felt across Canada.

11. Labrador was severely (affected/effected) _____ by the Spanish flu epidemic of 1918–19. One (affect/effect) _____ was the loss of more than 25% of its coastal population.

12. Gordon Campbell was the premier of British Columbia (whose/who's) _____ decision to introduce the HST caused his party to drop in the polls.

13. In Canada, the (principal/principle) _____ significance of the 1923 Halibut Treaty lies in its status as the first international treaty to have been signed by Canadian rather than British statesmen.

14. Kate Middleton (accepted/excepted) _____ the marriage proposal of Prince William in the fall of 2010.

15. Every Canadian prime minister (accept/except) _____ Kim Campbell has been male.

16. The Royal North-West Mounted Police together with the Dominion Police turned (into/in to) _____ the RCMP.

17. The stolen goods were turned (into/in to) _____ the RCMP.

౼ ANSWER KEY ౼

1. their
2. two
3. which
4. cannot
5. all right
6. there
7. anti-
8. were
9. its

10. that
11. affected; effect
12. whose
13. principal
14. accepted
15. except
16. into
17. in to

CHAPTER 10

REVISING AND EDITING

This guide is not a history cookbook, for the simple reason that there are no recipes for writing history. There are conventions, of course, but every historian has his or her own way of writing. Approaches to any given project depend partly on personal style and partly on the subject of the work. The more you write, the stronger your sense of your own style and interests will become. At the same time, you will become more familiar with your own strengths and weaknesses. You have probably heard of the ancient Greek inscription over the temple at Delphi: "Know thyself." Get to know your weaknesses as a writer; then watch out for them.

GET SOME PERSPECTIVE ON YOUR DRAFT

Once your **draft** is completed, it's important to get some distance from it before you begin the revision process. Try to spend a few days working on other things. If you don't have days to spare, even an hour doing something else will help you to see your paper as your readers will, with fresh eyes.

If you're lucky, you may have an instructor or friend who would be willing to read a first draft and comment on it. Take any critical comments seriously. Early comments on a draft can help you determine whether you have made a persuasive case.

THINK ABOUT A TITLE

Now that you have finalized your argument, you can start thinking about a title. The best titles are not just informative but also intriguing. One student, writing a paper about an ancient Egyptian queen who, on the death of her husband, declared herself king, chose the title "She's the

Man: An Analysis of Hatshepsut's Reign." The subtitle alone would have been an adequate title, but the touch of humour made the full version more effective. Another student, writing about the film *Schindler's List*, entitled it "The List Was Life and the List Was Good, but Was the Movie? A Historical Analysis of *Schindler's List*." Again, the subtitle would have been enough, but a bit of a yawn. The full version, with its subtle allusion to the creation story in the Bible, was more likely to catch a reader's attention. In both cases, the title gave some insight into the point of the paper.

REVISE YOUR DRAFT

A critical reader will assess both the strengths and the weaknesses of your paper. Sometimes it is difficult to take criticism, but the best critics spend a great deal of time thinking about your work. This in itself is a compliment. Even if you conclude that some unfavourable comment was mistaken, the criticism will have had the positive effect of making you reconfirm your position.

Now that you have some perspective on your writing, it's time to begin revising. First address your critic's comments, which may concern both the style and the substance of the paper. Write another draft that incorporates the suggested changes. Then stand back and assess the paper again. Have you addressed your critic's comments fully?

No critic, no matter how generous, will tell you everything you need to know in order to turn your draft into a prize-winning piece of writing. You yourself must take responsibility for revising. One basic strategy is to begin with broad revisions to the arguments and narratives before tackling the details of sentences and word choice. Finally, you will need to proofread for spelling, grammar, punctuation, and formatting.

EVALUATE YOUR OWN ARGUMENTS AND NARRATIVES

The key components of historical argumentation were outlined in Chapter 6. Check your writing thoroughly for the following points. Does the evidence support the inferences? Are all the inferences fully warranted? Does the argument develop logically? Does it flow? Will readers find it interesting and significant?

Chapter 7 outlined the key components of historical narratives. Check your writing to make sure that your audience knows what they need to know in the correct order. Are terms, characters, and events introduced clearly? Are events presented in chronological sequence? Have you included all the relevant dates? Is there any extraneous information that does not belong in any of the main stories? Have you established a consistent voice as a narrator?

EVALUATE YOUR SENTENCES AND WORD CHOICES

This book has already offered some advice on how to write sentences and how to choose the right words. While you are revising, you need to stand back and look at your sentences as your readers will. Have you chosen strong verbs? Is the order of ideas appropriate? Does every sentence follow logically from the one before it and develop a new idea?

Also look at your word choices as your audience will. Is your language free of jargon? Have you defined all the specialized terms that readers may not be familiar with? Is there anything that readers are likely to find pretentious?

PROOFREAD THE FINAL DRAFT

Proofreading is an essential part of writing history. If your writing is sprinkled with mistakes, no matter how minor, even your most brilliant work will look like a comedy of errors.

Proofreading takes time and patience. Chances are that by the time you start, you will already know parts of the paper so well that your eyes will start to wander. Be disciplined. It's easier to spot mistakes on paper than on screen, so print out a copy and force yourself to read every word. When this gets too boring, put the paper aside for a short time and come back to it later. You might even try reading the pages in reverse order, so that you focus on the words rather than the argument and narrative. There is no way to make proofreading interesting, but it has to be done.

PROOFREAD FOR PUNCTUATION

When their work is criticized specifically for poor punctuation, history students sometimes complain to their professors that "This is not an English course!" True enough. However, history is mostly a written discipline, and those who can't communicate in writing will not succeed. Proper punctuation is not a frill: it is an absolute necessity. Look at the following two sentences quoted in a recent bestseller:

> A woman, without her man, is nothing.
> A woman: without her, man is nothing.[65]

Changing the punctuation changes the meaning entirely. It's said that during a heated debate in Britain's House of Lords, one member insulted another. The insulted lord demanded an apology and the offending lord replied: "I called the Right Honourable Lord a liar it is true and I am sorry for it. And the Right Honourable Lord may punctuate as he pleases."[66]

Misunderstandings caused by imprecise punctuation are probably more common than you think. If you have trouble with punctuation, refer to Turabian or the *Chicago Manual of Style* for guidance. Many other writing manuals discuss punctuation as well.

PROOFREAD FOR SPELLING

Spelling errors can be the most embarrassing of all mistakes. (Or was that embarassing? Are you sure?) For that reason it's essential to use the spell-checking feature on your word-processing program. Just remember that spell-checkers don't think and are incapable of catching all spelling mistakes. In particular, they are not designed to catch mistakes involving homophones: words that sound the same but mean different things, such as "thrown" versus "throne," or ""reign" versus "rein" versus "rain." As long as a word exists in the spellchecker's dictionary, it will not be recognized as an error, even if it makes no sense at all in the context of your paper. After running the spell-checker, therefore, you need to print out a hard copy and recheck it yourself.

CHECK FOR CONSISTENCY

Many historians in Canada prefer English to American spelling: "colour," for example, rather than "color," "centre" rather than "center." Others don't care much, and many teachers will be happy to accept papers written in either style. It's important to be consistent, though. The best way to avoid mixing styles is to choose one dictionary and follow its spellings for all such words. If in doubt about which style to use for a particular course, ask your instructor.

DOUBLE-CHECK POSSESSIVES

Chances are that if you are learning to write history, you have already learned how to write a grammatical sentence. Even so, there is a type of grammatical error that is embarrassingly common even among professional historians. It involves the formation of the possessive, and most of the confusion surrounds words that end in the letter *s*.

1. *Form the possessive of a singular noun by adding 's.* This rule holds even when the word ends in the letter *s*, as in "Cecil Rhodes's diamond mines," or "the duchess's letters."

    There are some minor exceptions to this rule. Traditionally, ancient names ending in *s* have taken only an apostrophe, as in "Moses' laws," "Jesus' name," or "Herodotus' histories." Since these constructions are somewhat awkward, however, many writers prefer to use *of* to form the possessive in such cases: "the laws of Moses," for instance, or "the name of Jesus."

2. *Form the possessive of a plural noun by adding an apostrophe.* This is true when the plural is formed by adding an *s*, for example, "the Redcoats' muskets" or "the Wright brothers' airplane."

3. *Don't use an apostrophe with initialisms or numbers.* It used to be standard practice to use an apostrophe to form the plural of initialisms (terms such as MP, CEO, or PC) and numbers: for example, "PC's were first manufactured during the 1980's." Most style manuals now recommend omitting the apostrophe in such cases: "PCs," "1980s." Use an apostrophe only when there is the

possibility of confusion, as in "There are two o's and two p's in apostrophe."

4. ***Never use an apostrophe to form a plural.*** Columbus did not discover "the America's." He discovered "the Americas" (at least some people think he did).

CHECK YOUR FORMATTING

Professors sometimes have their own preferences regarding formatting and paper presentation. Pay careful attention to any instructions you are given. If you have not received any specific directions, make sure that you have used a consistent word-processing format throughout the paper. A consistent format is crucial because aberrations are distracting. Your readers will also expect a simple format. Typically, history professors prefer a 12-point plain font with one-inch margins and lines double-spaced. Be sure that the pages are numbered, and that your name and the paper's title are on the first page. Some professors may also ask for a title page. This should include your name, the professor's name, the course name or number, and the date of submission, as well as the paper's title. While you are checking the format of the hard copy, be sure to check the elements that do not necessarily appear clearly on screen when you are writing, such as footnotes, margins, and page numbers.

READ YOUR PAPER ALOUD

Reading aloud is the oldest trick in the book for catching writing problems because it forces you to review every word. It should be the last thing you do before you submit your work. You may be surprised to find that you will hear mistakes that you did not see on the printed page. Your roommate may think you're eccentric, but your readers will appreciate the end result: a better piece of writing.

SUBMIT YOUR PAPER

Before submitting your paper, take one last look through to be sure everything is there and in the correct order. Fasten the pages securely according to your professor's instructions. Be sure to make a copy of the finished product. Professors rarely misplace papers, but it can happen, and it will make your life considerably easier if you have a replacement copy on hand. Be sure to keep absolutely all of your notes, drafts, and any other in-process materials in case your professor asks to see them. Then submit your paper with pride, knowing that you have done your best.

✍ REVIEW ✍

1. Take a break to give yourself some perspective.
2. Choose a meaningful title.
3. Ask someone else to read your paper and comment on it.
4. Revise, revise, revise—everything from arguments to spelling and punctuation.
5. Check and re-check.
6. Keep all notes and drafts.
7. Make a copy and save it!

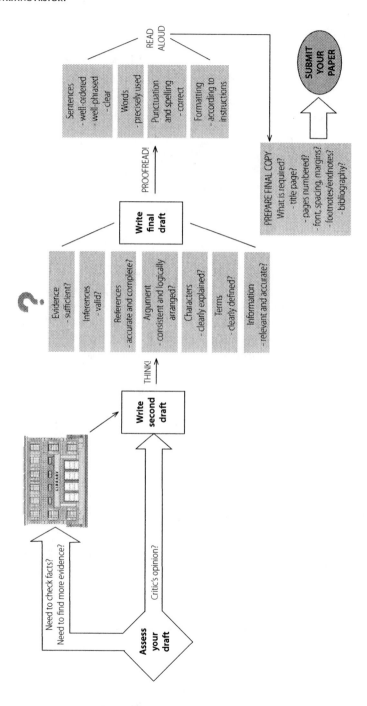

READ ALOUD

Sentences
- well-ordered
- well-phrased
- clear

Words
- precisely used

Punctuation and spelling
- correct

Formatting
- according to instructions

PROOFREAD!

Write final draft

?

Evidence
- sufficient?

Inferences
- valid?

References
- accurate and complete?

Argument
- consistent and logically arranged?

Characters
- clearly explained?

Terms
- clearly defined?

Information
- relevant and accurate?

THINK!

Write second draft

Need to check facts?
Need to find more evidence?

Critic's opinion?

Assess your draft

PREPARE FINAL COPY
What is required?
- title page?
- pages numbered?
- font, spacing, margins?
- footnotes/endnotes?
- bibliography?

SUBMIT YOUR PAPER

✍ CHAPTER 11 ᧑

OTHER ASSIGNMENTS

Most of this book is concerned with helping you to prepare and write the most frequently assigned project in a post-secondary history course, the research paper. Instructors do also assign other types of projects, however. The specifics vary, but most of these other assignments rely on the same basic techniques that are discussed throughout this book: library research, checking and analysis of sources, careful documentation, and so on. As always, pay close attention to your instructor's specific requirements and instructions, document your work carefully, and keep all your notes and drafts.

RESEARCH PROPOSAL

A research proposal, submitted before you begin writing, can be a very useful exercise. It gives you the opportunity to start work in good time, to think carefully about your topic, and to get feedback from your instructor, all of which will help you produce a strong final paper. Just keep in mind that such assignments are not as easy as they may look. Thoughtful and careful work now will make the writing process easier and will give your instructor a better opportunity to guide you. Allow yourself plenty of time. You will need to think about a subject, search out relevant sources, and read them in enough detail to know how they relate to your topic and to each other.

Generally, a research proposal will include a title, a short description of your research topic and its significance, a list (in proper bibliographical format) of the sources you intend to use and how you intend to use them, and a provisional thesis statement. The final paper may not conform exactly to your proposal, since your instructor's feedback and your own further research may lead you to new sources and ideas. The paper should not differ from the proposal too much, however, or the project will become meaningless.

ANNOTATED BIBLIOGRAPHY

This assignment may be either a "stand-alone" project or a first step towards an eventual paper. In the latter case, it is very like a research proposal except that it concentrates more on assessing the works in question than on discussing the paper's thesis or direction. You will still need to keep your thesis in mind, however, to make the most of the project and to ensure that your bibliography is coherent and focused, not just a random list of works.

For the assignment itself, you will likely be asked to propose a title or a topic for research. Be sure to present each book, article, or document title in proper bibliographical format. In each case, summarize the main points of the work and evaluate its major strengths and weaknesses. If required, explain briefly how you intend to use each work in your research paper.

BOOK AND ARTICLE REVIEWS

History students are frequently asked to review books or articles. Whatever form the material takes, your job is to summarize and assess it.

BOOK REVIEW

Historians frequently consult book reviews to find new work relevant to their area of study. Learning to write a useful review requires practice. A book review assignment allows you to gain this practice, as well as to become familiar with a specific subject and to hone your analytical skills. It goes beyond the scope of a book report, which is essentially an extended summary, to look at the book's theme and purpose, its evidence and arguments, and its conclusions and significance. If you have never written a book review, you may find it helpful to look at examples in scholarly journals such as *The Canadian Historical Review* or the *Canadian Journal of History.*

The first step is obvious: read the book. There is no substitute for careful and thoughtful reading of the entire work, although it is definitely useful to scan the introduction, chapter headings, and conclusion up front. As you read, note the author's main points and your observations of the evidence or arguments, as well as any short passages that you may want to quote in your review.

Once you have read the book, you can plan your approach. Does the assignment require you to look at other sources so as to put the book into a wider context? Are you supposed to link this book to the themes or materials of your course, or simply to review it according to your own evaluation of its merits? If you do further reading, pay attention to matters relating to "your" book's main arguments and evidence, especially if other sources emphasize significant ideas or events that your book seems to skim over or ignore. Don't let yourself get sidetracked by details that are insignificant or unrelated to the book's main arguments. Also think about the criteria you will use to evaluate it. Your personal response to the book—what you liked or didn't like about it—is not irrelevant, but your responsibility as a reviewer is to judge the strength of its arguments and evidence, identify its strengths and weaknesses, and assess its usefulness. If you have some knowledge of the subject from other sources, you can think about how this book fits in: does it generally agree, disagree, offer a new perspective? If you are evaluating the book on its own merits, try to place it in the context of the themes and materials you are studying in your course.

When your reading and research are complete and you have decided on the main points to discuss, you are ready to begin writing. Be sure to follow your instructor's guidelines regarding length and presentation. Typically, a review will begin with a bibliographical reference that lists the author, title, and publication information for the work under review. Unless you have been instructed otherwise, summarize the work briefly, being careful to focus on the main points and the relevant evidence. Include a thesis statement that makes your overall opinion of the book clear. This would also be a good place to mention the author's background and qualifications: whether he or she is a professional historian, has specific expertise in the area, or has written other books on this or related subjects. You could also mention the arrangement of the book's contents, any additional features such as illustrations, and the style of writing. Keep these details brief, though; you want as much space as possible for substantive discussion of the book's contents.

The body of the review will present your assessment of the book's arguments, evidence, and conclusion. Consider whether the author has achieved his or her goal and whether you are convinced by the arguments. You may include some quotations from the book, as long as they are short, relevant to your point, and representative of the book's contents, tone, and ideas. Just be sure not to take any quotation out of context—otherwise you run the risk of misrepresenting the author's meaning—and never quote anything just for the sake of quoting.

The last component of any book review is the conclusion. In this paragraph, summarize your main points, give your overall assessment of the book, and (if appropriate to the assignment) make a recommendation to your reader.

Throughout the writing process, remember that your job is to give your readers a clear, balanced idea of the book as a whole. Don't focus on one area of the work while ignoring other equally significant areas. And don't feel that you have to find something negative to say in order to fulfill your role as a critic. . No book is perfect, and it's perfectly legitimate to note flaws if you find them, but you should be equally ready to praise the book's strengths. Finally, be sure to back up both your praise and your criticism with specific examples.

COMPARATIVE BOOK REVIEW

A second type of book review assignment requires you to compare two or three different books. If your professor leaves the selection of works to you, look for books on topics that bear some relationship to one another. Once you have found some likely candidates, take a quick look through them to be sure there is a real basis for comparison. Two biographies of Louis Riel would obviously work well for this type of essay. But one on Riel himself and one on Canadian federal policy towards First Nations peoples in the nineteenth century might also allow you to make some useful commentary. Writing a coherent comparison of a book on Riel and a book on women in the fur trade would be a much tougher job.

Once you have selected your books, go through them and note any points of similarity or difference, agreement or disagreement. Are there any areas where one book sheds light on the other? When you have finished your careful reading you can decide which points are significant and which can be ignored. For example, suppose you were reviewing Reinhold Kramer's scholarly biography *Mordecai Richler: Leaving St Urbain* in tandem with Joe King's popular history *From the Ghetto to the Main: The Story of Jews in Montreal*. King's portrait of the novelist's home community—which he fled as a young man and returned to in middle age—might give you some additional insight into the Richler portrayed by Kramer, who places his subject in the context of a changing Jewish culture in Montreal and the world. A comparative review of King and Kramer might also allow you to comment on the differences between popular and scholarly history.[67] Of course you won't be able to discuss everything the two authors say: just pick out the most significant areas. Now you can consider how to organize your review.

Start as before, with full bibliographical references, an introduction, and a short description of each book. Now there are two ways to proceed: you can discuss each book in its own section and then compare some of their points, or you can organize your paper thematically and compare the books directly, point by point. One way to choose between these approaches is to consider how directly the two works can be compared. If you have books with related but not identical subjects, can you find more than one or two significant elements to compare directly? If not, it might be easier to go with option number one. If you can find significant points that are directly comparable, then you might choose option number two.

ARTICLE REVIEW

A third very common review assignment concentrates on one or more articles as opposed to books. The overall task is the same, but you will most likely be given fewer pages to work with. In this case it is crucial to keep your summary of the articles short so that you have adequate space for analytical comments.

HISTORIOGRAPHICAL PAPER

Historiography is the study of how history is written—in effect, how historians shape history through their work. Thus a historiography paper generally takes a topic that has generated continuing interest and explores how historians have written about it.

History is not static. Interpretations of the past change because, as John H. Arnold points out:

> History is above all else an argument. It is an argument between different historians; and, perhaps, an argument between the past and present."[68]

Historians do not generally strive for "the right answer." They strive to interpret the available evidence as fully and accurately as they can. Even when working with exactly the same evidence, their opinions frequently differ. Thus when Robin Fisher's re-examination of sources led him to portray the indigenous peoples of the Pacific coast as savvy traders who were fully capable of holding their own against Europeans, he challenged the standard interpretation and stimulated a flurry of new interest and new opinions on the subject. In other words, he started an argument, in the best intellectual sense of the term—which is exactly what new research ought to do.

Historians' interests and approaches also reflect their own times and circumstances. In the 1960s and 1970s, historians responded to the growth of feminist activism with a new interest in the history of women as a separate topic from the history of men. More recently, with the discussion of gay rights in Canada, interest in "queer" history has increased. Recent years have also seen growing interest in local history and the history of childhood.

What kinds of subjects might be suitable for a historiographical paper? You could look at the historiography of a theme such as the development of the Canadian labour movement, an event such as the Oka Crisis of 1990, or a person such as Louis Riel or Prime Minister Mackenzie King. Any topic that has been controversial or that historians have revisited in different ways over time would be suitable. It is also possible to write a historiographical paper about a particular historian, tracing the development of his or her work.

Typically, a historiographical paper will focus on how historians' approaches, themes, and questions have developed over the years and from place to place, providing insight into the historians and their times as well as the historical topic under discussion. Look for continuing or recurring themes, new themes and reassessments of old themes, agreements and disagreements. The point is not particularly to review or critique the works or historians in question, although you could well include some comments along these lines. Rather, the point is to examine change over time, to explore how and why historians' methods, interests, and approaches have changed. A chronological organization usually works well for historiographical papers, but you could modify this format to discuss sub-themes such as the influence of gender or ethnicity on the writing of history.

PRIMARY DOCUMENT ANALYSIS

Primary sources are not limited to documents: they can include any sort of physical object from the era under study, from burial sites and gravestones to household items and coins to photographs and works of art. Although all of these are well worth studying, in this section we will focus on documents. Among the primary documents that professional historians rely on are letters, diaries, newspaper accounts, government documents, legal papers, tax statements, and church records, to name only a few. Instructors often set document analysis assignments to give students an opportunity to conduct primary research and get a stronger feel for the times under study than secondary sources can give.

Primary documents can be tricky to read if they are written in archaic or extremely formal language. Have a good dictionary close by and use it to look up anything you don't understand. If the document is very old, you may need to consult the full-length *Oxford English Dictionary* (as opposed to the various shorter and "concise" editions), which gives the history of a word's usage as well as current meanings. The complete *OED* runs to 20 volumes, so you will need to find it in a library or (by subscription) online.

Primary document analysis demands that you bring your critical abilities to bear. All such documents, public as well as private, were produced by real people who were influenced by the times and places in which they lived, as well as their own experiences. This means that you need to keep the context in mind as you read. What your instructor will be looking for is not simply a summary of what the document says, but a thoughtful analysis of what it means and what it can tell us about people, places, and events. The simplest way to approach document analysis is to follow the "question" model outlined in Chapter 2. You won't always be able to answer every question suggested here, and sometimes the answers—the whys and hows, or the wheres and whens—will overlap. Still, posing the questions will help you to think carefully about your document.

The "who" question. Who wrote the document? What do you know (or what can you find out) about the author(s)? How does this person's background or experience help to explain his or her point of view? Was the author personally involved in, or affected by, the events discussed in the document? Looking at it from the other side, what does the document tell you about its author? What can you say about his or her values or outlook on the basis of the document?

The "what" question. What is this document? Is it official (say, a government report) or private (a diary entry)? What can you learn from it about the time and place in which it was written?

The "why" question. Why was this document written? Was it intended to influence others, or to express a personal point of view? Did the author want to influence events to come, or to explain events that had already occurred?

The "when" question. When was the document written? Was it contemporary to the events it discusses or describes? If not, was it written before or after the events? Does this chronological relationship make a difference to your understanding of the document? To your assessment of its value or validity?

The "how" question. How was this document produced? How was it supposed to be used? How was it actually used? How was it preserved, and does that make a difference to your assessment of the document?

ORAL HISTORY PROJECT

Traditionally, historians have relied on written sources, but in recent decades they have become increasingly aware of the limits that this approach imposes. Before reasonably modern times, for example, most people were unable to read or write, and therefore they could not leave written accounts of their existence or experience. Written records thus reflected the interests and views of the literate minority, politicians and those in power, and the voices of the majority were for the most part either ignored or viewed through the eyes of the powerful and educated. In addition, there are many peoples (Canada's Aboriginal peoples among them) whose histories have been transmitted orally rather than in writing. Oral history techniques have provided essential insights into people whose lives and experiences otherwise might be lost to history. Oral history is a subfield of history, and it has its own guidelines. You can find handbooks and guides from around the world at the Canadian Oral History Association's website (www.canoha.ca/reference/links). One very useful starting point included on this site is UCLA Berkeley's "The One-Minute Guide to Conducting Oral History."

Personal interviews can give fascinating insight into some topic areas. For instance, if you were planning a paper on the Canadian forces in the Second World War, perhaps you could interview a veteran of the Normandy landings. If you know a doctor who specializes in the treatment of stress disorders, he or she might be able to give you some valuable insights into the post-traumatic stress suffered by many soldiers. Interviewing people is one of the most exciting aspects of historical research.

If you find it difficult to ask someone for an interview, keep in mind that most people will be flattered to know that their life or work is historically significant. But an interview is more than just a conversation: it's a way to seek critical information about the past. Therefore you should be as systematic as possible in your interviewing. Here are some guidelines:

1.   *Do your homework.* Before you conduct the interview, learn all that you can from written sources. Then make a list of questions that you want to ask your subject. Try to make sure that you have all the background information you need, and that you have a clear idea of what you want to find out: otherwise, you will simply waste your subject's time as well your own. This doesn't mean that you should close off all avenues of discussion except those that you have determined in advance. It does mean that your work should have a point to it, and that this point should be clear both to you and to your subject. Otherwise, your subject may think that you don't know what you're talking about and may not trust you enough to give you much useful information.

2.   *Be sure to understand the legalities.* If you are a student, find out from your instructor whether your college or university has published ethical guidelines for conducting research on "human subjects." If this is the case, be sure to follow the guidelines. Graduate students, postdoctoral researchers and faculty members will almost certainly be obliged to follow the university's standards for research on "human subjects." You can find Canadian guidelines on the Oral History Association's website (above). You will probably need to obtain a signed release from your interview subjects indicating that they understand the terms of the interview arrangement and are willing to have their testimony used in the way you intend (see page 134 for an example of a release form). For example, are you planning to quote the interview in your paper? If so, your release form should say so.

3.   *Be considerate.* Pay attention to what your subjects tell you, if only through their body language. If they seem uncomfortable, try to figure out why. Then do whatever is necessary to accommodate them. For instance, if they don't want to be identified, *you must respect their wishes.* Perhaps they would allow you to identify them by code names or numbers.

     It's important to be honest when you are writing up an interview, but the feelings of the people involved are at least equally important. Never repeat hurtful material if it is not necessary or if it would compromise someone who is not involved with the interview. For example, if an interview subject is discussing some indiscretion or illegal activity in his youth and tells you the name of someone else who was involved, you should probably not repeat that name in your paper. If in doubt, consult your instructor before proceeding.

Remember also that your schedule is not important to your interview subjects; be prepared to conduct the interview at a time that suits them and in the place of their choice. People often prefer to do interviews in their homes, and this often is the best place, since you want them to be relaxed and open. In any case, do try to arrange for a quiet place where you won't be interrupted or distracted.

4. *Be patient.* It takes time to set up an interview, and you may have difficulty getting in touch with some subjects. It's often a good idea to have references on hand to offer potential subjects, or even to mail them a resumé and a brief description of your project. It may take two or three interviews before your subject trusts you enough to share interesting information with you. If you plan to interview people, start work on the project as soon as possible: that way you will have plenty of time to meet your deadlines.

5. *Take scrupulous notes.* Always take written notes during an interview. You may also want to use a tape or digital recorder, or even a camera, but outside noise can interfere, batteries can die, and the wrong buttons can get pressed. Back up your work with written notes. A recording device can also make a subject uncomfortable. If you notice that the device is interfering with the interview, turn it off and rely on your written notes. After you have completed each interview, transcribe the notes and give a copy to the subject. Also remember to send a note of thanks to every subject, as well as anyone who may have helped to set up the interview.

6. *Think critically about oral sources.* Information obtained through interviews is often reliable, but like all historical evidence it should be subject to critical evaluation. Be aware

that your subjects may not remember events exactly as they happened. If possible, compare their stories with the stories that other people tell you, as well as any written sources that may be available. Written sources are not necessarily more reliable than oral sources, but writing can often be a more effective way to preserve a version of history.

7. *Cultivate your skills both as an interviewer and as an interpreter of interviews.* It takes a lot of practice to learn how to work with interview subjects. The best interviewers are usually the most experienced, but even they were beginners once. For a thorough guide to the process, see Valerie Raleigh Yow, *Recording Oral History: A Guide for the Humanities and Social Sciences,* 2nd ed. (Toronto: Altamira Press, 2005). For a shorter guide that focuses more specifically on the practical details of oral history see Edward D. Ives, *The Tape-Recorded Interview: a Manual for Fieldworkers in Folklore and Oral History,* 2nd ed. (Knoxville: University of Tennessee Press, 1995).

Once your interviewing is complete, use the evidence you have gathered just as you would use any historical source—as long as the use is in accordance with whatever guidelines have been set in your consent form. Be respectful of your subjects' meanings and intentions.

READING RESPONSE JOURNAL

A reading journal assignment is designed to allow you to develop your own thoughts about course materials without the constraints that come with an essay assignment, although some instructors assign reading journals as bases for later papers. Unless otherwise instructed, you can use informal language and your own approach and arrangement, and you can let your thoughts run free. Keep some guidelines in mind, however. If your instructor is to read some or all of your material, keep your language clean, your thoughts focused, and your points clear. This assignment is about thinking, not random musing.

Briefly summarize the reading, making sure to identify the most important points, any contentious points, and any points you do not understand. If you are responding to more than one piece, think about any similarities and differences of focus and opinion and consider the reasons. Are the arguments or approaches valid?

If appropriate to the assignment, you might (within limits) consider your own reactions: for example, do you find the material interesting, dull, surprising, amusing, upsetting, intriguing? Why do you feel this way? Emotional responses can be interesting, and you may certainly include them (unless your instructor rules them out). However, responses based on historical knowledge, on other reading, or on experience are more relevant, and these are what your instructor will be looking for.

One final note: try to set aside a regular time for your journal. It may be tempting to let the journal slide when you have more immediate deadlines, but you will regret putting the journal work off when you have to catch up on it several weeks or months later. You will not be able to do a good and thoughtful job under those circumstances. Besides, the whole point of a response journal is to record your thinking as it develops over time and help you to consolidate your understanding of the materials as the course progresses. Writing several weeks' worth of journal entries all at once defeats the purpose and deprives you of the benefits. Another advantage of diligent journal work will become obvious when you have to prepare for papers and exams. A carefully completed journal, with good summaries of course readings, will save you a great deal of effort later on.

ESSAY EXAMS

Most history exams include an essay component, and a little planning can help you a lot. Listen carefully in class for any clues your instructor gives in the few weeks before exam time: many drop hints for those who are paying attention. Try not to leave your studying until the last moment. Set aside a regular time to study and review, and keep to your schedule. This will be far more useful than any last-minute cramming. Watch for recurring themes, ideas, people, or events frequently emphasized by the book or instructor.

An especially useful study method is to compose your own essay questions and then write model answers to them. For example, if a major course theme has been the development of federal–provincial relations in the nineteenth century, you could compose a question about the shifting power dynamics between the two levels of government. Then you could decide on and study the major "sign-post" events and factors to discuss, such as the rise of the provincial rights movement, the Ontario boundary dispute of the 1880s, the North-West Rebellion, the formation of the *Parti national*, the Manitoba schools question, and the Laurier–Greenway compromise. Your question will probably not be identical to anything on the exam paper, but you will almost certainly have studied in detail the material necessary to answer your instructor's questions.

When writing the exam, read each question carefully and think about what a thorough but focused answer needs to cover. Take a few moments to write a brief outline. Remember that every essay requires an introduction and conclusion, a thesis statement, logical ordering of points, and sufficient evidence to support your arguments. Focus on the question in front of you: don't try to change it into a question you can answer more easily, and don't pad your answer with a lot of unnecessary information just because you know it. You need to show your instructor that you understand the material so well that you are able not just to regurgitate but to develop your own thoughts based on all the evidence. Be aware of any constraints of time or length and try to leave a few minutes to proofread, to make sure that both your ideas and your handwriting are clear.

PRACTICAL STRATEGIES

No matter what type of exam you are taking, it will go better if you have a strategy. Obviously, you are more likely to do well if you have worked hard all term and studied diligently for the exam. Apart from any other benefit, this will give you the confidence you need to get a good sleep the night before the exam and arrive well rested. "All-nighters" rarely produce good exam results.

Also make sure you know what you are allowed to bring to the exam. Scrap paper? Something to drink? Should you take a sweater? Tissues?

Will you be allowed a bathroom break? Prepare beforehand so that you won't be distracted during the exam.

When you get the exam, don't just jump in and start writing. Take a few moments to read it carefully. Pay attention to any directions regarding the length or format of your answers. As you read, think about how much time you have and assign a ballpark time limit to each part of the exam so that you will not feel overly rushed. First, identify the easiest questions and if you can answer them very quickly, do that now. If there are some that will be easy but will need a little time to compose, set them aside for now.

Next, look at the rest of the questions. If you think some will be really difficult, set them aside as well and just let them percolate in the back of your brain for a while. You may find that, as you relax into the exam, you will start remembering things that you thought you had forgotten. In the meantime, complete first the questions that are neither the easiest nor the hardest. Then go back to the easy ones, but resist any temptation to spend too much time or space on the answers just because you know them so well. Finally, turn to the hardest questions. Following this approach allows you to use your time effectively and ensure that you don't leave any "easy" marks on the table.

Above all, have confidence and remember that an exam is a chance to show how much you know. Your professor will be looking for the correct answers to straight factual questions, of course, but also for evidence that you have thought about the material and made it your own. If you really have worked properly all semester, you might even find that you enjoy writing the exam.

↩ REVIEW ↪

1. Most history assignments use similar techniques and approaches.
2. Prepare carefully for exams: don't try to cram.
3. Relax—you know this stuff!

ANYPLACE UNIVERSITY

Two copies of this form are required.
One signed copy of the form is to remain with the interview subject.
A second signed copy must be submitted to the course instructor.

Student Interviewer and contact information _____

Course for which the interviews are taking place _____

Course instructor and contact information _____

Participant _____

I agree to be interviewed by_____ as part of his/her research for _____ (course) at Anyplace University. I understand that the information from the taped/transcribed interview will be used as part of the research material for _____'s paper in _____ course at Anyplace University. I do ☐ /do not ☐ give my permission for one copy of any tapes, transcripts or photographs made during this project to be deposited in the library or archives of Anyplace University and used by undergraduate ☐ , graduate ☐ , and faculty researchers ☐ , and the public ☐ for educational purposes including research papers ☐ , publications ☐, exhibitions ☐, World Wide Web ☐, and presentations ☐. (Check all that apply)

By giving my permission, I do not give up any copyright or performance rights that I may hold.

My participation is voluntary and I may refuse at any time to participate further. One copy of the tapes/transcripts of my interview(s) will be given to me. Except as provided above, all other copies will be_____ after the course is completed.

Further restrictions (if any) on the use of the materials:

_____

_____

_____

_____

_____

I am of legal age to provide consent.

_____
Signature of Participant and date

_____
Signature of Interviewer and date

Figure 11.1 Interview release form

❧ APPENDIX ❧
ESSAY CONCEPT MAPS

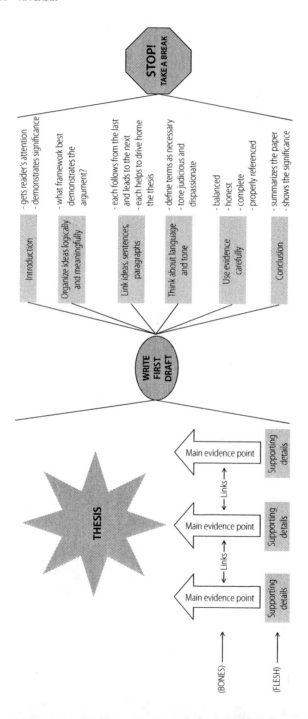

STOP!
TAKE A BREAK

Introduction
- gets reader's attention
- demonstrates significance

Organize ideas logically and meaningfully
- what framework best demonstrates the argument?

Link ideas, sentences, paragraphs
- each follows from the last and leads to the next
- each helps to drive home the thesis

Think about language and tone
- define terms as necessary
- tone judicious and dispassionate

Use evidence carefully
- balanced
- honest
- complete
- properly referenced

Conclusion
- summarizes the paper
- shows the significance

WRITE FIRST DRAFT

THESIS

Main evidence point

Main evidence point

Main evidence point

Links

Links

Supporting details

Supporting details

Supporting details

(BONES)

(FLESH)

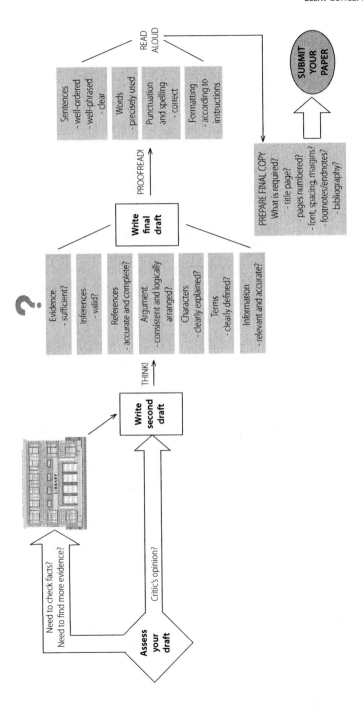

✐ GLOSSARY ✐

The numbers in parentheses refer to the pages where the terms are first used. All terms are defined here as they are used in this book.

analytical essay (44): An essay that examines an analytical problem (e.g., the relationship between science and culture). An analytical essay uses short narratives to shed light on the concept or problem under examination.

annotated bibliography (19): A list of sources that includes not only the publishing information but a brief description of each work.

archival material (10): Historical material, typically artifacts and primary documents, stored in archives.

argument (18): In a court case, the lawyers for each side argue their case—that is, they present their interpretation of the evidence—in such a way as to persuade their audience (the judge and jury). Like lawyers, historians frequently dispute one another's arguments.

bibliography (5): A list of the books, articles, and other documents on which an author has relied. All the relevant publishing information, including author (and/or editor), title, place and date of publication, and publisher, must be included.

block quotation (53): A quotation that is longer than three lines, set off from the main text in its own indented block, without quotation marks.

citation system (60): The particular system used to cite sources in a given work. Historians typically use the "Chicago" or "Turabian" system, based on footnotes (or endnotes) and bibliographies. Other citation systems include MLA and APA, both of which use parenthetical referencing within the text.

citation (50): A reference note. Most citations include a specific page reference

cliché (102): A trite, overused phrase; for example, "in the nick of time."

colloquial language (99): Informal or casual language, including slang and contractions; not appropriate for history papers.

database (8): An online collection of materials such as documents or journal articles that are useful in specific fields of study. Often available only through library subscription.

deduction (36): Deductive reasoning reaches reasonable conclusions based on sometimes limited evidence; the most likely explanation.

discursive note (67): A footnote or

endnote that serves some purpose other than source identification: e.g., to clarify or expand on some aspect of the text.

draft (71): An early version of a piece of writing. For an essay, you should expect to write two or three drafts.

ellipses (54): Three dots (...) inserted into a quotation to show where words have been omitted.

endnote (61): See **footnote.**

euphemism (101): An evasive word or phrase used to soften the message or avoid giving offence; for example, "follically challenged" used in place of "bald."

footnote (13): A reference note (flagged by a superscript number in the text) that identifies the source(s) on which a particular passage is based. Footnotes appear at the bottom of the relevant text pages; endnotes appear on separate pages at the end of the text.

historiography (1): The study of the writing of history; the study of the discipline itself.

hypothesis (18): The question or proposition that drives research on a specific topic.

induction (39): Inductive reasoning reaches generalised conclusions based on putting sometimes many pieces of evidence together.

inference (30): A conclusion based on the examination of evidence.

jargon (97): Technical or specialized words or phrases; generally inappro-priate for use outside a specific professions or groups.

narrative essay (46): An essay that may include analytical points but focuses on telling a single chronological story and generally arrives at one major conclusion.

paraphrase (51): A rewording of a source's statement in roughly the same number of words (a shorter rewording is a summary).

peer review (16): Pre-publication review of a book or article by one or more professionals in the field to assess its accuracy and credibility and make recommendations for revisions. Articles published in scholarly journals are generally peer-reviewed.

plagiarism (50): The use of someone else's words or ideas without proper acknowledgement.

popular history (13): A book or article written for the general public rather than for a scholarly audience.

primary source (14): A source written or created in the time period under study; a first-hand account.

scholarly history (13): History written for a scholarly audience, particularly other historians. Scholarly history is usually based on original research and contributes new information or interpretations to the field. Such works have generally undergone rigorous peer review and editing.

secondary source (15): Typically, a book or article based on primary sources. The works written by historians are generally secondary sources.

summary (51): A concise restatement of a source's discussion, argument, etc.

superscript number (61): A small number written or printed above the line of text and used for referencing purposes. Each number corresponds to a footnote or endnote in which the author lists all the relevant publication and other information as necessary. Most word processing programs today have automatic footnote or endnote functions, usually accessed through "insert."

thesis (28): The central point that a piece of historical writing sets out to maintain or prove; usually introduced early in the work in a "thesis statement."

transition sentence (74): A sentence that connects one part of an argument with another; typically used to end one paragraph or begin the next.

✏ NOTES ✏

1. Margaret MacMillan, *The Uses and Abuses of History* (Toronto: Viking Canada, 2008), xi.
2. Peter Novick, *That Noble Dream: The "Objectivity Question" and the American Historical Profession* (Cambridge: Cambridge University Press, 1988), 7.
3. Thucydides, *The Peloponnesian War*, trans. Rex Warner (New York: Penguin Books, 1954; repr. 1984), 145.
4. Ruth Sandwell, ed., *To the Past: History Education, Public Memory, and Citizenship in Canada* (Toronto: University of Toronto Press, 2006), 10.
5. Arthur J. Ray, *"I Have Lived Here Since the World Began": An Illustrated History of Canadian Native People*, 3rd ed. (Toronto: Key Porter, 2010).
6. *The American Historical Association's Guide to Historical Literature*, 3rd ed., ed. Mary Beth Norton and Pamela Gerardi, 2 vols (New York: Oxford University Press, 1995).
7. *Canadian History: A Reader's Guide*, M. Brook Taylor and Doug Owram, eds., 2 vols. (Toronto: University of Toronto Press, 1994); Norah Story, *The Oxford Companion to Canadian History and Literature* (Toronto: Oxford University Press, 1967); and the *Supplement to the Oxford Companion to Canadian History and Literature*, ed. William Toye (Toronto: Oxford University Press, 1973). *Introducing Canada: An Annotated Bibliography of Canadian History in English*, ed. Brian Gobbett and Robert Irwin (Lanham, MD: Scarecrow Press, 1998). *Canadian Reference Sources: An Annotated Bibliography*, comp. and ed. Mary E. Bond (Vancouver: University of British Columbia Press, 1996). *Canadian Reference Sources* also includes works in French.
8. *Annual Bulletin of the Historical Association* (UK: Blackwell, for the Historical Association, 1997–present).
9. Diana Pedersen, *Changing Women, Changing History: A Bibliography of the History of Women in Canada* (Ottawa: Carleton University Press, 1996). George P. Murdock, *The Ethnographic Bibliography of North America*, 4th ed. (New Haven: Human Relations Area Files, 1975); and the *4th edition Supplement 1973–1987* (New Haven: Human Relations Area Files, 1990). Owen A. Cook, *The Canadian Military Experience 1867–1995: A Bibliography* (Ottawa: Department of National Defence, 1997). Barbara J. Lowther, *A Bibliography of British Columbia: Laying the Foundations, 1849–1899* (Victoria: University of Victoria, 1968). Linda Hale, *The Vancouver Centennial Bibliography* (Vancouver: Vancouver Historical Society, 1986).
10. *The Canadian Encyclopedia* (Edmonton: Hurtig, 1985, 1988 and online at www.thecanadianencyclopedia.com) and *The Canadian Encyclopedia: Year 2000 Edition* (Toronto: McClelland & Stewart, 1999). *The Dictionary of Canadian Biography*, 15 vols. (Toronto: University of Toronto Press and Les Presses de l'Université Laval, 1966–2005). (Note that *The Dictionary of Canadian Biography* is also available online through the Library and Archives Canada website at www.collectionscanada.ca/index_e.html). Gerald Hallowell, ed., *The Oxford Companion to Canadian History* (Toronto: Oxford University Press, 2004). The new *Oxford Companion* does not simply replace or update the older version, which is now a bit elderly but still useful. The new *Companion* contains an encyclopedic series of short articles on a vast

number of Canadian history topics. *The Encyclopedia of Canada's Peoples,* ed. Paul Robert Magosci (Toronto: University of Toronto Press, 1999). *Canadian Who's Who* (Toronto: University of Toronto Press) has been published annually since 1910. It can be found in microfiche for the years 1898–1975, on CD-ROM since 1997 and also online at www.utpress. utoronto.ca/cww. *The Canadian Annual Review of Politics and Public Affairs* (Toronto: University of Toronto Press) contains synopses of each year's affairs. It is published several years after the fact, so that the volume published in 2006 covers up to 2000. The *Fitzhenry and Whiteside Book of Canadian Facts and Dates,* ed. Richard W. Pound, 3rd ed. (Markham, ON: Fitzhenry and Whiteside, 2005) is a basic list of events and people from "the making of a planet" through 2003, and it also contains a bibliography section.

11. R. Cole Harris et al., eds., *The Historical Atlas of Canada,* 3 vols. (Toronto: University of Toronto Press, 1987–1993) and William G. Dean et al., eds., *The Concise Historical Atlas of Canada,* (Toronto: University of Toronto Press, 1998).

12. H.V. Nelles, *A Little History of Canada* (Toronto: Oxford University Press, 2004).

13. Heather Robertson, *Measuring Mother Earth: How Joe the Kid Became Tyrell of the North* (Toronto: McClelland and Stewart, 2007).

14. Hippocrates, *Precepts,* as quoted by Chester W. Starr in *A History of the Ancient World,* 3rd ed. (New York: Oxford University Press, 1983), 331.

15. For a broader discussion of these research questions, see Richard Marius and Melvin E. Page, *A Short Guide to Writing about History,* 6th ed. (New York: Pearson/Longman, 2007), 32–9.

16. Wendy Wickwire, "To See Ourselves as the Other's Other: Nlaka'pamux Contact Narratives," *Canadian Historical Review* 75, 1 (1994): 1–20.

17. Loren R. Graham, *The Ghost of the Executed Engineer: Technology and the Fall of the Soviet Union* (Cambridge: Harvard University Press, 1993).

18. Walt Whitman, "The Real War Will Never Get in the Books," *Specimen Days* (New York: Signet Classic, 1961), 112.

19. Deborah E. Lipstadt, *Denying the Holocaust* (New York: Penguin, 1993).

20. John H. Arnold, *History: A Very Short Introduction* (Oxford: Oxford University Press, 2000) 13.

21. Cole Harris, *The Resettlement of British Columbia: Essays on Colonialism and Geographical Change* (Vancouver: University of British Columbia Press, 1997).

22. Prasenjit Duara, *Culture, Power, and the State: Rural North China, 1900–1942* (Stanford: Stanford University Press, 1988). Philip C. C. Huang, *The Peasant Economy and Social Change in North China* (Stanford: Stanford University Press, 1985). Ramon Myers, *The Chinese Peasant Economy: Agricultural Development in Hopei and Shantung, 1840–1940* (Cambridge: Harvard University Press, 1970).

23. Gerald L. Geison, *The Private Science of Louis Pasteur* (Princeton: Princeton University Press, 1995), 149–56.

24. James Fairhead and Melissa Leach, *Misreading the African Landscape: Society and Ecology in a Forest-Savanna Mosaic* (Cambridge: Cambridge University Press, 1996).

25. Jan Vansina, *Living with Africa* (Madison: University of Wisconsin Press, 1994), 16–17.

26. Robin Fisher, *Contact and Conflict: Indian–European Relations in British Columbia, 1774–1890* (Vancouver: University of British Columbia Press, 1977; 2nd ed. 1992).

27. Jules David Prown, "Mind in Matter: An Introduction to Material Culture

Theory and Method," in *Material Life in America, 1600–1860*, ed. Robert Blair St. George (Boston: Northeastern University Press, 1991), 17–35. Thanks to Elizabeth Abrams for suggesting this article.

28. Charles S. Maier, *The Unmasterable Past: History, Holocaust, and German National Identity* (Cambridge: Harvard University Press, 1988), 1.

29. John Mack Farragher, *A Great and Noble Scheme: The Tragic Story of The Expulsion of the French Acadians from Their American Homeland* (New York: Norton, 2005), 473.

30. Georges Lefebvre, *The Coming of the French Revolution*, trans. R.R. Palmer (Princeton: Princeton University Press, 1947; rev. ed. 1989).

31. Betty Jo Teeter Dobbs, *The Janus Faces of Genius: The Role of Alchemy in Newton's Thought* (Cambridge: Cambridge University Press, 1991), 10.

32. Samuel Eliot Morison, "History as a Literary Art: An Appeal to Young Historians," *Old South Leaflets* ser. 2, no. 1 (Boston: Old South Association, 1946): 7.

33. Cicero, *Pro Publio Sestio*, 2.62. As quoted by John Bartlett and Justin Kaplan, eds., *Bartlett's Familiar Quotations*, 16th ed. (Boston: Little Brown, 1992), 87.

34. These suggestions are taken from Gordon Harvey, *Writing with Sources* (Cambridge, MA: Harvard University, 1995), 27–9.

35. Cole Harris, *The Reluctant Land: Society, Space and Environment in Canada* (Vancouver: University of British Columbia Press, 2008), 16.

36. Maurice Basque, "Family and Political Culture in Pre-Conquest Acadia," in *The Conquest of Acadia, 1710*, John G. Reid, Maurice Basque, Elizabeth Mancke, Barry Moody, Geoffrey Plank and William Wicken (Toronto: University of Toronto Press, 2004), 49.

37. J.R. Miller, *Lethal Legacy: Current Native Controversies in Canada* (Toronto: McClelland and Stewart, 2004), 118–119.

38. "'The Declaration of the Reformers of the City of Toronto to their Fellow-Reformers in Upper Canada, Toronto, August 2, 1837,' The Constitution," in Colin Read and Ronald J. Stagg, eds., *The Rebellion of 1837 in Upper Canada: A Collection of Documents* (Ottawa: Carleton University Press, 1985), 60.

39. Margaret MacMillan, *Paris 1919: Six Months That Changed the World* (New York: Random House, 2001), 45.

40. Harvey, *Writing with Sources*, 21–3.

41. Colin M. Coates, "Commemorating the Woman Warrior of New France, Madeleine de Verchères, 1696–1930," in *Gender and History in Canada*, ed. Joy Parr and Mark Rosenfeld (Toronto: Copp Clark, 1996), 130.

42. Harvey, *Writing with Sources*, 13–16.

43. *Chicago Manual of Style*, 15th ed. (Chicago: University of Chicago Press, 2003). See also Kate L. Turabian, *Student's Guide to Writing College Papers*, 4th ed., rev. by Gregory G. Colomb, Joseph M. Williams and the University of Chicago Press editorial staff (Chicago: University of Chicago Press, 2010).

44. Jean Barman, "Taming Aboriginal Sexuality: Gender, Power, and Race in British Columbia, 1850–1900," *BC Studies*, No.115/116 (Autumn/Winter 1997–1998): 237.

45. Roger Gibbins and Loleen Berdahl, *Western Visions, Western Futures: Perspectives on the West in Canada*, 2nd ed. (Peterborough, ON: Broadview, 2003), 25–63.

46. My thanks to Justin Elsworth for the use of "Britannia Beach: A Microcosm of British Columbia" (History 205 paper, Capilano College, 2008), 2–3. Note that I have slightly modified the text, for clarity when taken out of context, and that the original included references.

47. A.I. Sabra, "Situating Arabic Science: Locality versus Essence," the History of Science Society Distinguished Lecture, published in *Isis* 87, no. 4 (December 1996): 654–70. Quotation from p. 668.

48. William Cronon, *Changes in the Land: Indians, Colonists, and the Ecology of New England* (New York: Hill and Wang, 1983), 6.

49. Carl Degler, *In Search of Human Nature: The Decline and Revival of Darwinism in American Social Thought* (Oxford: Oxford University Press, 1991), vii.

50. Robert Jay Lifton, *The Nazi Doctors: Killing and the Psychology of Genocide* (New York: Basic Books, 1986), 341, 378.

51. Afua Cooper, *The Hanging of Angélique: The Untold Story of Canadian Slavery and the Burning of Old Montreal* (Toronto: HarperCollins, 2006), 14.

52. Robert S. McElvaine, *Eve's Seed: Biology, the Sexes, and the Course of History* (New York: McGraw-Hill, 2001), 26–32.

53. Mercedes Steedman, "The Red Petticoat Brigade: Mine Mill Women's Auxiliaries and the 'Threat from Within,' 1940s–70s," in *Canadian Working-Class History: Selected Readings*, ed. Laura Sefton MacDowell and Ian Radforth, 3rd ed. (Toronto: Canadian Scholars' Press, 2006), 327.

54. Herodotus, *The Histories*, trans. Aubrey de Sélincourt (New York: Penguin Classics, 1954; rev. ed. 1983), 519.

55. Starr, *History of the Ancient World*, 294–5.

56. Franklin W. Knight, *The Caribbean: The Genesis of a Fragmented Nationalism*, 2nd ed. (New York: Oxford University Press, 1990).

57. Christopher Hibbert, *The Great Mutiny: India 1857* (New York: Penguin Books, 1978), 63.

58. John Demos, *The Unredeemed Captive: A Family Story from Early America* (New York: Vintage Books, 1994), 146.

59. Hibbert, *Great Mutiny*, 24.

60. Hibbert, *Great Mutiny*, 388.

61. Winston S. Churchill, *The Birth of Britain*, vol. 1 in *History of the English-Speaking Peoples* (New York: Dodd, Mead, and Co., 1956; Bantam, 1974), 131.

62. *Bartlett's Familiar Quotations*, 16th ed., p. 620.

63. James Belich, *The Victorian Interpretation of Racial Conflict: The Maori, the British, and the New Zealand Wars* (Montreal and Kingston: McGill-Queen's University Press, 1989), 20–1.

64. George Orwell, "Politics and the English Language," in *Fields of Writing*, ed. Nancy Comley et al., 4th ed. (New York: St. Martin's Press, 1994), 618.

65. Lynn Truss, *Eats, Shoots & Leaves: The Zero Tolerance Approach to Punctuation* (New York: Gotham Books, 2004) 9.

66. Mary Refling et al., Postings to the H-Albion bulletin board, 8–10 July 1997, http://h-net2.msu.edu/,albion.

67. Reinhold Kramer, *Mordecai Richler: Leaving St. Urbain* (Montreal and Kingston: McGill-Queen's University Press, 2008). Joe King, *From the Ghetto to the Main: The Story of Jews in Montreal* (Montreal: Montreal Jewish Publication Society, 2001).

68. Arnold, *History*, 13.

⚙ INDEX ☙